Essential Tips for Classroom Success

Also by Doug Campbell
*Discipline without Anger: A New Style of
Classroom Management*

Essential Tips for Classroom Success

365 Ways to Become a Better Educator

Doug Campbell

ROWMAN & LITTLEFIELD
Lanham • Boulder • New York • London

Published by Rowman & Littlefield
A wholly owned subsidiary of
The Rowman & Littlefield Publishing Group, Inc.
4501 Forbes Boulevard, Suite 200, Lanham, Maryland 20706
https://rowman.com

Unit A, Whitacre Mews, 26-34 Stannary Street, London SE11 4AB,
United Kingdom

Copyright © 2018 by Doug Campbell

All rights reserved. No part of this book may be reproduced in any form or by any electronic or mechanical means, including information storage and retrieval systems, without written permission from the publisher, except by a reviewer who may quote passages in a review.

British Library Cataloguing in Publication Information Available

Library of Congress Cataloging-in-Publication Data Available

ISBN 978-1-4758-3391-1 (cloth : alk. paper)
ISBN 978-1-4758-3392-8 (pbk. : alk. paper)
ISBN 978-1-4758-3393-5 (electronic)

∞ ™ The paper used in this publication meets the minimum requirements of American National Standard for Information Sciences Permanence of Paper for Printed Library Materials, ANSI/NISO Z39.48-1992.

Printed in the United States of America

This book is dedicated to Betty Harper, my supervising teacher during my student teaching assignment at Hillcrest High School in Simpsonville, South Carolina. Thanks for believing in me, Mrs. Harper.

I would also like to thank my parents, who could have easily flipped out when I told them that all of that money they spent on college was going to go toward a teaching degree instead of a law degree like I had originally planned.

Last but not least, this book is for every teacher who ever felt stressed out, lost, or unprepared for the challenges that come with choosing a career in education.

Contents

Preface ix

1 Discipline 1
2 Mental Health 41
3 Wellness 63
4 Success 69
5 Wisdom 85
6 Relationships with Students 93
7 Relationships with Other Teachers 111
8 Relationships with Administrators 119
9 Relationships with Parents 125
10 Advice for Administrators 129
11 Discipline Myths 141
12 Coaching 153

Conclusion 159
About the Author 161

Preface

After twenty plus years in the classroom teaching mostly high school math, I have learned one lesson more than any others: teaching is hard. Some parts of it are obviously difficult—every teacher knows going in that there is the possibility of misbehaving students, cranky bosses, and tough coworkers. I am not sure that future teachers really know *how* hard teaching is, though.

It is one thing to be aware that students might misbehave, but until you are faced with the situation, it is really difficult to know what it is like—and how hard it can be to handle and "fix." There are also other challenges connected to finding success, protecting your health (both mental and physical), and getting along with the various kinds of people you have to deal with in an education career (students, parents, administrators, other teachers, etc.).

So as I look back on my teaching career and its ups and downs, I realize that some of the lessons I learned may be useful to other teachers. Some of these lessons I learned from making mistakes, some I learned from others, and some I learned from taking initiative and studying the secrets of success for various aspects of the teaching profession.

After working in education for so long, I can honestly say that I have seen a lot. There are not many things that would surprise me. This is not to say that I have done everything and been through everything. Far from it. But I can safely say that I have seen enough that I am able to share some insights that may be of use to teachers and other educators, no matter if you have been teaching for thirty years or if this is your first year teaching.

I know about the long hours, the inevitable stress, the lack of appreciation, and the general grind that comes from teaching the same group of students and working with the same group of adults day after day over the course of a given school year. I also know about the fantastic relationships that can be formed along the way, the feeling of accomplishment, and the great sense of satisfaction that teachers can feel at the end of the school year—knowing that they did their best to make an impact on the lives of young people.

As part of the agreement that I made with my publisher when writing my first book, *Discipline without Anger* (Rowman & Littlefield, 2012), I created a website and blog as a part of the promotion for the book. If you have never blogged before, coming up with blog topics can be a challenge. So I decided to start a series of tips for teachers. The list turned into a series of 101 tips about discipline and general teacher survival. Teachers are busy, and I figured that the short and easy format of a tip and a paragraph or two would be perfect for their needs.

The blog series worked well, and when I completed my list of 101 tips, I realized that I had a lot more tips in me! So I kept blogging. I kept writing them down and keeping track of them in my phone as I thought of them. For the next few years, I kept myself aware of possible tips as I observed my own situations in the classroom and talked to other educators. I really wasn't doing this with much more of an agenda other than to keep the blog going. I just kept paying attention, writing down tips, and moving on. Well, during a recent summer break, I decided to compile my list and see how many tips I had up to that point. I realized that I had come up with about two hundred more tips!

At this point, I realized that I might have enough for another book. And this, my friends, is what you now see before you. So here they are: 365 tips. Tips about everything from discipline, classroom management, relationships at school, and general success and survival in the honorable profession of educator. I hope you find something useful!

Throughout the book, I've included an occasional "Story Time" section after some of the tips. These are simply quick stories from my teaching career about the inspiration behind the advice I am giving. I hope you enjoy them.

Chapter One

Discipline

Discipline almost seems to be a dirty word these days. It doesn't have to be. As Mr. Clark says in the movie Lean on Me, *"Discipline is not the enemy of enthusiasm!" Discipline (and its close cousin "classroom management") sometimes seem to get a bad rap because of the people who do it poorly. Most teachers would probably agree that students need boundaries. That is all discipline is—setting boundaries and using consequences to correct misbehavior. It can be done out of cruelty or hate, or it can be done out of love. Parents who never discipline their children usually are ones who don't really care. So teachers who care can discipline too. The trick is to figure out the best ways to do it fairly and effectively in a classroom setting.*

1. Make classroom management a priority.

This is true for all teachers but especially for those who are new to the profession. Teaching is hard. Anyone who has ever taught knows this. And yet it seems that many teachers do not fully realize the importance of classroom management. There is more than one way to do it successfully, but you would be wise to try to get it figured out as soon as possible.

Try to figure out a style of discipline that works for you. Read books, blogs, and websites on it. Ask other teachers. Do whatever it takes to figure out exactly how you want to go about it. Even if you disagree with everything in this book about classroom management and discipline, do yourself a favor and make sure you do *something*. Being casual or unprepared could have extremely bad results and even ruin your teaching experience.

2. Love your students unconditionally.

Let's face it, some students are nice, and some aren't so nice. Some may like you, and some may hate you. People are different. However, if you want to be a successful teacher in the long run (and keep your peace of mind), there is one rule that you absolutely must follow: you have to love your students. Period. Do they insult you? Talk about you behind your back? Intentionally annoy you? Say they hate you and your subject? Teach long enough and all of these things will happen. It doesn't matter. Make up your mind to love your students no matter what they do and who they are, and you will be much more effective, impactful, and happy.

3. Be unemotional when giving consequences.

This is one of the most important points in this entire book. So much is written about the strategy behind the specifics of consequences, but the case can be made that *the way* they are given is equally important, if not more so. Let your consequences stand on their own. Give them out almost like you are just keeping track instead of using them like some kind of weapon in an angry moment. In most cases, you should not feel a need to add attitude or anger.

The best way to achieve this goal is to have your consequences established ahead of time. If you are careful to make them reasonable, you can then be at ease to just let the consequence speak for itself. If you feel like you have to add anger or intimidation to them, that may be a sign that you don't feel comfortable enough with their effectiveness.

Whenever you give a consequence, think of yourself as the scorekeeper. If you are playing football and you give up a touchdown, the scorekeeper does not yell at you as he is putting six points up on the board. That is just the result of your action. Even referees throwing a flag for unsportsmanlike conduct do not get an attitude about it. They simply announce the penalty and assess the yardage and continue the game. That is how consequences should be given.

Some might say that you should stop everything and have a discussion about why the action of the student was wrong and why they should stop doing it. This is probably going overboard in most cases. Unless a particular misbehavior is unusual in some way, most students know that they have done wrong and why. Just give them the consequence they brought on themselves and move on.

4. Keep a discipline record.

This doesn't have to be anything fancy. Just do something to keep track of your students' misbehavior. Keeping a record will not only help you be able to communicate better with parents, but it will also help you stay aware of students who are misbehaving in a consistent but not extreme way. Accumulation of steady misbehavior may not be at the top of your list of concerns, but it is something that may be helpful to know.

5. Don't overdo rewards.

Some teachers seem to think that bribing their students is a great discipline idea. They may say something like, "Be good for a week and we will have a party on Friday!" or something similar. While this strategy may work at first, it will almost inevitably fall apart in the long run. The problem with this method is that students will eventually get tired of the reward. In order to keep it interesting, you will have to keep raising the stakes and making the rewards better and better. A little reward incentive here and there is not the worst thing in the world, just don't depend on it as your main method of classroom management.

Story Time: My first teaching job was with a mostly self-contained class that was called "transition." This was a class for ninth graders who were moved out of middle school for being too old, even though they hadn't really passed. Most of these students were too old because they had spent time in a juvenile detention center. Not the friendliest environment to teach in. By the end of the year, about half of the class had either been kicked out of school or returned to the detention center.

I was learning classroom management on the job with this class. They basically became my personal discipline experiment. I tried anything I could to find that magic tactic that would work best. A couple of months in, I thought I had found a winning idea. I set up a reward system in which students would get some kind of treat for good behavior. I made a poster for the wall, kept track of each student, the whole deal. It worked beautifully. The class behaved so well that I thought I had found the secret of behavior management. A substitute teacher who covered my class even told me how great the system worked. This lasted for all of about two weeks. After that, the students were mostly back to their normal disruptive behavior. So, be careful about relying too much on bribing your students to behave for you. Your system will either run out of steam, or you will find yourself having to continually increase the value of the rewards.

6. Model good manners.

Manners seem to be vanishing from society in general. Make a contribution to the overall good and insist that your students use them in your classroom (things like saying please and thank you, yes sir and yes ma'am, not interrupting, picking up things people drop, etc.). There are many valuable things that teachers can teach other than the content required for their subject. Manners and etiquette are two of those things.

Also, manners are much more valuable than just creating a pleasant classroom. Soft skills like manners, etiquette, and class can help prepare students for more success in the business world, personal relationships, and general well-being.

So what is the best way to teach manners in the classroom? Being clear about your expectations is a good start. This is also an area where what you do may be more important than what you say. If you require your students to have good manners and then don't have them yourself, that behavior will be much harder to enforce. Create a positive, welcoming vibe in your classroom. This starts by having and expecting civilized behavior.

7. Don't try to be cool or popular.

This advice is certainly nothing new in the teaching profession. The logic is simple: worrying about being popular can easily lead to a lack of authenticity, compromise, and a big no-no for teachers—favoritism. The best thing you can do is figure out how to be yourself and work that into the framework of what you want to accomplish in the classroom. If you happen to be a "cool" type of person, great. Be yourself (within the boundaries of professionality and good taste, of course). Just don't try to fake your coolness. Students can spot that a mile away, and they will crush you for it.

8. Sweat the small stuff.

There is a somewhat common (and damaging) attitude among teachers that they should only worry about the big stuff. "Everything is fine as long as the students aren't killing each other or fighting or doing anything dramatically bad," someone might say. This is a mistake. There is obviously logic in this way of this thinking, and yes, if nothing terrible happens in your classroom on a given day, then that is somewhat of a victory in itself. You can aim higher than that, though. Sometimes the best thing you can do is not to always let little things go.

There are two main reasons that teachers should sweat the small stuff—in other words, not let little things go. First, there are many *small* types of misbehaviors that can have a very large negative impact on learning. Talking when the teacher is talking, for instance, or being too loud during reading time are examples of misbehaviors that may not seem like much of an emergency. If they are disrupting or slowing down learning in any way, though, they should not be allowed.

Also, there is something about paying attention to the little things that makes students think twice about major misbehaviors. The thinking goes that if the teacher takes things that small so seriously, the students should be terrified to find out what will happen if they do something really bad. This may seem a little sneaky, but it often works. The further away you draw the line of bad behavior, the closer students will come to crossing that line. If your line is just don't cuss, do drugs, or fight, then you will be opening the door to a lot of disruptive behavior.

9. Don't automatically believe students' excuses.

Of course, every student is an angel and would never do anything mischievous or dishonest. But just in case you run into a rare situation where a student tries to get something over on you, it is good to be prepared. As nice as it would be to be able to trust everything every student ever tells you, this is just not a realistic idea. Let's face it, some adults are deceitful and dishonest, so it makes sense that some kids may be as well.

To be clear, this is not to suggest that you have to be paranoid and worry that every student is out to get you. Most kids, like most people, are generally good. This is just a warning to keep your guard up in case something fishy might be going on.

10. Don't tolerate disrespect.

Just like the general population, every student will not necessarily have an automatic respect for people. This is an unfortunate reality. It is best to know how you want to handle these situations before they occur. If you try to wing it, you will likely just go with your gut reaction and do one of two things: (1) blow up at them and get angry and mean or (2) brush it aside out of a fear of not looking "nice."

We all want to be liked and loved, but be sure that you don't let students cross too far over the line of disrespect. This is not to say that you should automatically send every student who looks at you funny to the principal's office, but you also don't want to let certain behaviors go. Even if your only consequence is simply voicing your disapproval, make sure you do *something* when a student shows disrespect. Tolerance of bad attitudes and disrespect toward teachers is a poison that can take over a class and even a school if it is allowed to run free.

11. Don't get overconfident with your classroom management skills.

There is a major risk involved for people who follow my tips: you may get so good that you get sloppy! This tip must be included for those of you who have great classroom management, whether you get it from this book or some other source. Maybe you are just a natural. However you became great at classroom management doesn't matter. Just be careful about getting complacent with your great skills. You never know when something may come up for which you are not prepared.

12. Act slightly crazy.

Don't get too carried away with this one, but would it really be a bad thing if there was some doubt in your students' minds about your sanity? It might make them think twice about messing with you.

13. Don't argue with students.

This can be a hard one. It can be so easy to fall into a reactive mode with students and argue with them. Do whatever you can to keep this from happening. Arguing almost always just makes you look bad as the authority figure. Make your case, be clear, and even listen to what a student has to say. Just don't let it regress into an ugly verbal confrontation. You may not realize it, but students are watching everything you do. Getting into arguments is a good way to lose credibility.

14. Don't tolerate bullies.

Nobody likes a bully. Most people have had to deal with them at some point in their lives. There is something about the strong pushing around the weak that gets under my skin. Thankfully, awareness of bullying has increased in recent years, and teachers are being trained to prevent it. Be on the lookout for even the slightest hint of bullying, and take a strong stance against it immediately. You don't have to pitch a fit or implement your most extreme consequence. Just be ready to nip it in the bud and eliminate it from your classroom and school as quickly as possible. Let students know that you take bullying seriously, no matter what form it takes.

15. Young teachers—make yourself look older.

A lot of teachers who are just starting out in their teaching career honestly don't look much older than the students. The truth is, they often aren't! They may be twenty-two or so teaching seventeen- and eighteen-year-olds. It is obviously not a good thing for students to think of their teacher as a peer, so do whatever it takes to look older. Switch from contact lenses to glasses. Grow a little facial hair. Dress up a little more for work. The method is not what is important here. Do whatever works for you. But taking a few small steps here and there to make yourself look more "adultish" can go a long way toward establishing your authority in the classroom.

16. Pick your battles.

Some things are worth fighting for, some are not. This is true no matter the situation. So be aware of what you are letting get to you or what you are willing to dig your heels in for. This advice applies to situations with students, administrators, parents, and even your own self-evaluation. Did a student break one of your rules or misbehave in some way that can be ignored and still be okay? You may want to just let it go. Did your boss do something that you didn't like? It happens. The important thing to ask yourself is if the issue is something that is worth fighting. Yes, some things should be addressed no matter what. If you really think about it, though, you may realize that some battles are better off left unfought.

17. Balance praise and criticism.

There seems to be a growing trend in education (and parenting for that matter) to strive to *only* be positive with kids. Cater to whatever they want. Don't ever correct them or say anything negative. Praise, praise, praise. Yes, this may be a bit of an exaggeration but not by much.

While a strict diet of positivity with kids may sound sweet and friendly, the result will more likely be a spoiled brat. The opposite is not good either. If all you do is criticize and correct kids, you will not be a good influence. So what is the secret? You guessed it. You should try to *balance* the positive and the negative. Have a little of both. Be truthful with students. Let them know when they are doing well and when they aren't doing well. Not only will they respect you more for it, but your words will be more believable as well.

18. Have a little swagger.

Teachers are authority figures. They may have a wide variety of personalities and styles, but they are still in charge. It is important that teachers act like they know what they are doing and act like they have a decent knowledge of what they are teaching. You may call this swagger, confidence, or self-belief. Just act like you belong.

Having confidence is important not only for discipline but also for the peace of mind of your students. It is a lot easier to listen to someone if you think they are an expert. And notice I said have a *little* swagger. That doesn't mean act like you are some perfect superhero or some egotistical jerk. Just show enough confidence to make students believe that you know what you are doing. And when you do mess up, be casual about it and don't act like it is the end of the world.

19. Don't try to copy another teacher's discipline style completely.

All teachers have their own style and personalities. Some are absolutely masterful at classroom management and keeping students on task. Be careful about trying to completely copy anyone, though. Something that works for them may be a disaster for you. It's okay to borrow ideas from other teachers, but be careful about trying to completely transform yourself into someone else. Not only will it likely not work for you, but it is also a good way to wear yourself out quickly. The faster you find your own style, the better off you will be.

20. Risk being disliked.

The temptation for a teacher to be popular is strong. Everyone likes to be liked. This is a matter of priorities, though. It comes down to your purpose for being there. Are you there to make friends? To be comforted? To have your ego stroked? Or are you there to serve your students? If your purpose is to do what is best for students, then that should come above all else. That may mean you have to risk being unpopular or disliked. Students are not always going to love everything you do or have them do. They may even hate you for it. This is just a risk you have to take. Usually, by the end of things, students can tell if you really have their best interests in mind.

21. Normalize future stressful events.

Students are going to face difficult times. If your class is challenging enough, it may be the most challenging thing they have ever done. Good. Don't try to pretend like this isn't the case. Letting students know ahead of time that things are going to be tough or difficult can help soften the blow. Giving a hard test? Tell them that it is going to be hard. Are they going to work extremely hard for that class? Tell them on the first day. Don't get all Pollyanna and sugary just because you want to come across as nice and positive. Whatever difficulty students are going to be facing in the future will be a little easier to take if they know it's coming.

22. Be willing to go against your natural reaction.

Let's face it, sometimes our natural reaction isn't always the best reaction. When students get mad or raise their voice at you, it may feel natural to get mad right back at them. A disrespectful student may give you the urge to answer with your own disrespect. Be careful. Most of the time, the best reaction to bad behavior like that is a calm response. So do yourself a favor and be aware that whatever feels "right" at the time may not always be the best course of action. If needed, use extreme self-control, and know that being under control is always best.

23. Don't be afraid of potential student misbehavior.

The fear that students will misbehave may be one of the biggest stresses that teachers face. The reason this is so stressful is not just the fear of the behavior itself but also the fear of not knowing how to handle it.

Kids are kids. You know that they are most likely going to be mischievous occasionally. So instead of starting every day with the fear that your students might act up in some way, *expect* it. Maybe you will be pleasantly surprised and they will act like angels and you won't have to deal with anything. Or maybe not. When you are prepared for the possibility of bad behavior and ready to deal with it, the fear becomes much less powerful.

24. Lightly "needle" students with behavior problems.

This tip can be a little risky, so use it at your own risk. The truth is that some students actually respect you more when you "mess" with them a little. This is not true of all students, so you have to be really careful about who you use this strategy with. Interestingly enough, this strategy works best with the students with the worst attitudes, as well as with the honors students. When you tease them a little, you are showing that you aren't overly impressed or intimidated with their extremely bad (or good) behavior.

Also, if you do it right, having fun with a student shows that you like them. We don't usually kid people who we don't think a lot of. This can be a powerful tool for relationship building. Just be careful who you use this strategy with. Try it with the wrong person and you could make someone mad at you.

25. Don't be a control freak.

Teachers are notorious for being control freaks, and honestly, having a knack for being in charge is not necessarily a negative thing in this profession. You may have been accused of being a control freak because of your rules, discipline, style, and so on. But this isn't necessarily true.

Discipline can be good, and it can be bad. It can be done out of anger, or it can be done out of love. The important thing is how you handle it. The key to not being a control freak with your rules and consequences is to have a reason for doing everything you do. If your rule system is based entirely on what is best for students, you don't have to worry about being controlling. On the other hand, if you have rules just because you like to be in charge, that is controlling. So watch your motives. Have your students' best interests in mind and you should be okay.

26. Be the adult.

If you teach children, it is important that you remember that you should be the mature one in the room. It is okay to cut up, have fun, smile, and so on, but still be sure that you don't cross the line of getting childish or immature. Be the adult. Be the leader. Your students will feel safer and more comfortable if you do.

27. Have a healthy mind-set about teaching.

Why did you get into teaching in the first place? Was it for the summers off? Good luck with that if that is all that is keeping you in the profession. Hopefully, you got into teaching to serve, help, and love students. It can be easy to lose sight of those motivations when you get into the daily grind of teaching. Sometimes reminding yourself and putting things in perspective can help you get over some of the little stresses of the day.

28. Don't be shocked by anything students do.

This tip is kind of depressing, but sex, drugs, violence, and other kinds of questionable behavior are all going on with more students than you may realize. Don't assume that every student who looks "bad" is bad, and don't assume that every student who looks "good" is well behaved. You may be shocked to know what some students are involved in. That does not mean that you should judge them or look down on them, just realize that people are not always what they seem to be. Students can often surprise you, for better or worse.

29. Be prepared for reasoning to not always be effective.

When students get mad or start to act up, their ability to reason will often disappear. Sometimes you just have to be blunt with your language and tell them exactly what you expect. Logic will not always work when you are trying to convince a student to do something, especially if things are getting heated.

30. Treat different ages differently.

Most teachers probably have about one or two age groups or grades that they work with best. If you are used to teaching seniors, you can't use the same methods with them that you would with freshmen. You can't teach second grade the same way you would fifth grade. And so on. Don't just have your cookie-cutter methods that you use for all classes, all levels, and all ages of students.

31. Act like you are fearless—even if you aren't.

There can be scary situations happening at school. Some are definitely scarier than others. It is important for teachers to try to do their best not to show fear during these times. This may sound overdramatic, but it is important that you do not show fear for a couple of reasons.

First, if you show fear of students misbehaving or intimidating you, you will have no authority in your classroom. Second, you can't be afraid of making mistakes in front of the class. Don't feel like you have to be some perfect superhero to be a good teacher. When (not if) you make a mistake, just correct yourself and handle it casually. A mistake is not the end of the world. Third, and maybe more important, students should feel safe in your classroom. In the unfortunate case that your students may be in danger, they need to look to you and see that you are calm and in charge.

32. Don't let honors students get away with bad behavior just because it's not "extreme."

Teachers of older students will often have a schedule that is a mixture of higher-level, honors-type classes, and lower-level, nonhonors classes. Let's be honest here, a lot of times the behavior in the nonhonors classes is worse than it is in other classes. These students often have not bought into the whole school thing, and as a result they don't feel a need to follow rules like other students might.

Because of this environment, teachers of these nonhonors classes often have a tendency to relax and loosen up when they have a class that does not behave poorly. Don't let this happen. Yes, it may be nice to have a class where students aren't always on the edge of fighting or cussing someone out or disrespecting you. These types of behaviors are not the only student behaviors that should be unacceptable, however. You should still hold these kinds of students accountable for "lesser" bad behavior like excessive talking, being rude to each other, and so forth. The lesser types of misbehaviors can often be much more common than major things, and they can ruin a learning environment just as easily. Don't let them.

33. Be prepared to deal with an ingrained general disrespect for authority.

Some people just don't like authority—kids and adults alike. It doesn't matter how nice or how reasonable you are, there are some people who will rebel at being told what to do. As a teacher, you should be prepared for these kinds of students.

Students who have this hatred for authority can express it in a variety of ways—they may calmly refuse to do what you ask them to do. They may get an attitude with you or disrespect you. Or they may even throw a full-on temper tantrum over things that may not seem like a big deal to you.

The best thing to do in these situations is to realize what is going on and not give up. There should be consequences of some kind for refusing to do what you ask students to do. Show them that you care about them and that you have their best interests in mind and you can often win them over. Be patient, and don't feel bad if these students don't return your positive energy for a while. A lot of times they will eventually either completely get on your side or they will at least realize that kind of behavior won't be tolerated in your class.

34. Don't take bad behavior personally.

This tip is very important, but it can also be extremely difficult to accomplish. A lot of teachers take bad behavior from students as a personal insult. While this may occasionally be true, it is more likely that there are other factors contributing to their behavior that have nothing to do with you. Keep this in mind so you can avoid lashing out or getting your feelings hurt the next time a student doesn't behave in your class. You will have a very long and stressful career if you are sensitive about every time a student misbehaves in your class. Developing a thick skin is one of the keys to long-term success in a career in education.

35. Be prepared to deal with grade worship.

Our system of education has created an environment where certain things seem to be out of whack. Educators are so determined to measure learning that the measuring tools (grades and test scores) have often become more important than the actual learning itself. Students have to pass tests to make it to the next grade. Schools have to meet a certain passing percentage to get funding or at least to avoid a bad reputation. College acceptance is dependent on certain tests. While it is true that grades and performance statistics have always been important, it seems like they are becoming more and more valued as time goes on.

What this system has created is an environment of grade worship. There is so much pressure on students, teachers, and schools to make certain grades or test scores that even educators can be capable of dishonesty, intimidation, or desperation to try to make sure they get the grade they want. Don't let this happen to you. Stay strong. Be committed to doing your best and helping students as much as possible, but don't allow yourself to cave into the pressure of cutting corners to try to be successful. Do things the right way or the next relevant statistic in your education career will be you.

36. Be prepared to deal with fights that start on social media.

Welcome to the twenty-first century. Remember the good old days when most student arguments would start on the playground? Well, those days are over, my friend. Students of all ages now have a public platform to start and fan the flames of their disputes. A lot of their drama plays out over Facebook, Twitter, SnapChat, or whatever else is the popular site of the day. As a result, intense arguments can be born and can often spill over into your classroom. Be aware of this possibility.

37. Establish your phone/technology expectations from day one.

People love their technology these days. A lot of schools are making their own school-wide policies forbidding things like cell phones and other electronic devices. If that is the case, you have it easy—just follow your school rule.

If you don't have a school policy to direct your stance on technology, you have to develop one on your own. Do you want electronic devices totally forbidden during your class? Used only at certain times? Do you want students to be able to use their devices whenever they want? Wherever you fall on the spectrum, it is wise to know how you want to handle it before the class starts. The worst thing you can do is to make a change in the middle of the term, especially if you are trying to move to a stricter policy. Establish your expectations in this area and stick to them.

38. Seat students alphabetically.

Seat students alphabetically for two reasons: (1) so you can learn their names faster and (2) so their papers are already in order when you collect them. This helps you enter and return papers faster, which is always a good thing. Seating students alphabetically also gives you an opportunity to tell them that you did not go around and ask other teachers who the bad kids are so you could seat them accordingly. Starting students out with a clean slate can be a good start to building a relationship with them.

39. Don't change a student's seat for behavior reasons.

Changing the talkative student's seat has long been a favorite consequence of teachers. Makes sense, right? Move the student away from the temptation and maybe they won't misbehave any more. But there is still something a little off about this strategy.

The lesson of responsibility for one's actions is one of the most important things that students can learn in school. As a result, you may want to try very hard to resist moving students' seats for behavior issues. They need to learn how to get along with people. It might be better for students to be left alone and to have to face your usual consequences than to be moved away from their seat to "save them" from misbehaving.

Also, changing a student's seat sends the message that you can't really handle them where they are. Now, if you have tried *everything* you can and students are still misbehaving, it is not the worst thing in the world to move them. Sometimes you have to do what you have to do. Just try to use this technique as one of your last lines of defense, not your first.

40. Enforce consequences quickly.

The reason for having consequences is to reinforce the correct behavior and motivate the student to avoid making the same mistake in the future. The longer you wait to enforce the consequence, the less likely the student will make the connection to the original behavior that needed changing. The best consequences are ones that you can give on the spot or at least on the same day. Much later than that and your consequence will have lost most of its effect.

41. Don't get personal when giving consequences.

It is very important that you show your students that you don't take their misbehavior personally and that it will not affect how much you like them. Do your best to send the message that the bad behavior is what you don't like, not the student.

42. Have private conversations with students about discipline issues.

Students *hate* being embarrassed in front of their peers. A lot of times that means that they will "bow up" on you if you call them out publicly, but they wouldn't if you had just talked to them privately. If you do choose to use this method, it is probably a bad idea to do it on a regular basis. Taking a student into the hallway for a private discussion should be the exception. If you do it too much, students are less likely to take you seriously.

43. Be slow to kick students out of class.

If your school has some kind of discipline system where you can send a student to the principal or some other kind of detention, be sure you are slow to send them out. Save that for extreme or excessive misbehavior, otherwise you will look like you can't handle your class. Sending students out too much or having unreasonably extreme consequences will quickly make you lose your reputation both with your students and administrators.

44. Don't assume all honors or private school kids will be angels.

Sometimes it seems like teachers get the idea that all lower-level kids are automatically rough and all honors-level kids are angels. Not so fast. *Both* groups can be full of plenty of misbehaving students, believe it or not. Sure, the way that students misbehave in both groups may look different, but both can still be plenty disruptive. Assuming that honors students will be perfectly behaved could make you complacent in setting up your discipline system. Have your classroom management plan set up and organized for them just like you would for a lower-level class. You never know what students are capable of.

45. Don't allow too much free time at the end of class.

Sometimes there may be a temptation to just give your classes excessive free time at the end of a period or day. You may be tired of working, and the students may be tired of working. Giving them a break makes sense, right? While it may sound good, this approach may not be such a good idea. For one, you only have so many minutes with your students in a given year. It is a finite amount of time, and you can never get it back. Also, idle time may inspire students to misbehave. So keep them busy when you can. And do your best to make that busyness productive.

46. Be willing to make changes to your discipline plan midyear.

Changing your discipline setup in the middle of a school year is not ideal. Classroom management is much easier to establish when it is consistent from day one. However, if you truly feel like there is a flaw in your system that you just have to change, don't feel like you are forced to keep it as is. Just keep your changes as simple as possible. This will help students adjust better to the changes, and it will make things easier for everyone.

47. Be careful how you handle group work.

Group work is a popular thing in education these days. It can be a great way for students to work and improve collaboration and social skills. If you are going to do group work, though, be sure that you are *very* structured and specific with your expectations. Group settings can be very tempting for students to let their minds and mouths drift away from the content being studied. You don't need to have it so organized that you turn your students into robots, just make sure that you are making your expectations very clear. Leave no room for wasted time.

48. Own the room.

Contrary to what some people may want you to believe, the teacher is the authority in the classroom. It's okay to act like it. This is not to say that you should go around acting like you are better than your students, just be sure to remember that you are in charge. Students need to know that there is someone confident and competent leading them.

49. Know how to handle times when you might be joining a class midyear.

Taking over another teacher's class is always tricky. You have no idea if he or she was strict, fun, outgoing, and so on. This is not the time to try to reinvent the wheel. Establish a few must-have, nonnegotiable rules, and don't try to shake them up too much. Do whatever you can to make the transition as smooth as possible.

50. Be willing to "accidentally" ignore some minor infractions.

This is one of those tips that is better off kept a secret from students, but it is probably best just to let some misbehaviors go. The specifics of the kinds of misbehaviors that you may want to let go don't matter. It may be different for different teachers. Remember, the point of discipline is not to catch students being bad. It is to establish boundaries in your classroom. So maybe sometimes it is better to just pretend you didn't see or hear some things every now and then. Your entire system of classroom management is not going to collapse if you do.

51. Know your school's discipline plan inside and out.

It may not seem this way, but teachers actually do not have unlimited power and control. Your school probably has some established rules about some things—big and small. You really do not want to be the type of teacher who goes all "rogue" and goes against school rules intentionally.

It doesn't really matter how much you like the rule or not. Do your job. Make your students follow the rules that your school establishes. Create your own rules where you can, and stick to the school rules where that is required of you. Don't give yourself a bad reputation with your administration by intentionally breaking school rules, and don't make your fellow teachers hate you when they make students follow rules that you aren't enforcing.

52. Don't assume students will be well mannered before they get to you.

Manners are important. In fact, they may be one of the most important things that students can learn at school. Yes, it would be nice if they were taught good manners at home. This doesn't always happen, though. The successful teacher tries to be aware of manners and uses mistakes in this area as teaching moments. Just be sure you teach manners from a place of respect and not one where you are getting fussy or judgy about it.

53. Get extremely calm if and when chaos occurs.

Every now and then you may find yourself in a chaotic situation in your classroom. A fight may break out or be about to break out. Students might get into an argument. Things may seem like they are about to completely fall apart. Instead of fearing the possibility of these situations, the best thing you can do is be prepared for them. A good rule to live by is that the more intense a situation gets, the calmer you should try to be. Now, sometimes it may take some yelling to stop an extremely tense situation. Most times, though, extreme calmness is a good antidote.

54. Keep a journal of your good discipline moves.

Have you ever had a great discipline day (or week or month or year) and wished you could remember exactly what you did to make things work out so well? Chances are that you don't remember every good idea you have ever had that worked in the classroom—especially when it comes to classroom management. Don't be stuck having to start over and over again with your discipline plans and mind-set. Keep a journal of what happens when you use certain strategies. At the very least, write down what you did when things go really well.

55. Don't "snap" at students.

If you just raise the level of respect you show your students, a lot of your discipline problems would be solved. Snapping at students is one way that some teachers try to establish control of their classroom, but it can really do damage to your relationships with your students. Do your best to handle consequences without getting angry or upset. Obviously, there may be times when you are so stressed out that you act in ways that you regret later. It happens. Just make it a goal to avoid making sharp, harsh comments to students and you will hopefully be in the right mind-set to be in full control of your emotions if things do get tense.

56. Don't display behavior records.

The logic behind posting a behavior chart is clear: when students see how their behavior compares to other students, they may face positive peer pressure to behave better. It may bring out a competitive spirit in you and inspire the entire class to raise their level of behavior. There is just something about this thinking that doesn't seem to fit, though. No matter how pure your intentions are, it is not fair to students to have their business made public. Yes, every student in class witnesses just about every misbehavior that occurs, and a chart keeping track of behavior would really be no surprise to anyone. That is not the point. The negativity from having a chart like this makes the harm it causes far outweigh the benefits.

57. Have one rule that is more strict than usual.

No matter what your discipline style is, it is probably a good idea to send a message to students that you can be strict if you have to be. The rule doesn't have to be anything outrageous. It can actually be something somewhat minor. Make your students stay until you dismiss them instead of just until the bell. Require them to ask permission to throw paper away. Be creative and find something that works for you.

The idea here is not to put on a display of your power. It is just to let students know that you have it if you need it. Is this overdoing things a little? Maybe. Just be prepared in case the misbehavior gets out of hand. Putting a little seed of doubt in students' minds is much smoother than having to make drastic changes in response to future bad behavior.

58. Don't give more than one warning before taking action.

Giving warnings without following through will make you the teacher who cried wolf—nobody will believe you. If you give a warning, make sure you follow through. If you don't, you will lose all credibility. The worst thing you can do is keep repeating yourself with no action.

59. Don't be afraid to use extra work as a consequence.

Teachers always seem to be searching for effective consequences. Some are definitely better than others. It can be easy to have a romantic notion that work in your subject area should never be used as a consequence. You don't want to turn a student off on your subject after all. This seems like an unlikely result, however. Also, desperate times sometimes call for desperate measures. While giving extra work may not be the best move to go to immediately, it probably shouldn't be eliminated from your bag of tricks either. At least establish the *possibility* that extra work may be coming.

In addition, this method probably works best when you have a group or entire class that is misbehaving. It is likely not the best strategy to use with individuals unless you have just tried everything else you can think of without any success.

60. Don't use writing sentences as a consequence.

Making a student write something over and over again is a classic consequence, so it must be effective, right? Not so fast. Yes, it does make the student uncomfortable, and they would probably rather not do it. There is just something too forced about it that makes this consequence ineffective in the long

61. Be willing to individualize rules if necessary.

You may occasionally have a student who repeatedly misbehaves in a way that doesn't officially break one of your rules. For instance, maybe a student talks and talks and talks and will not be quiet after repeatedly being asked to stop. It is okay to have an individualized rule for this student that he or she may not talk (even if it is during an activity where other students are allowed to do so). Don't have any fears that this may not be fair. The same thing applies to all students in your classroom. Individuals who continually cross the line and show no interest in changing their behavior may deserve their own set of rules and consequences, even if just temporarily.

62. Use short detentions as consequences.

Different schools have different rules when it comes to the kinds of consequences available to teachers. There is no one magic consequence that is going to solve all of your classroom management issues. A few smallish consequences to be given out before you get too serious may be helpful, though. Anything to give students a chance to turn their bad behavior around without anything extreme happening is always good. Short detentions are a great way to accomplish this goal. If you give the student a minor consequence and he or she *still* doesn't turn things around, though, at some point you have done all you can do. An extreme consequence may be the only option.

The idea behind consequences is to deter bad behavior. A lot of times this can be accomplished with something simply unpleasant. It doesn't have to be anything terrible and torturous. You might be tempted to think that consequences have to be *severe* to have any affect. I'm talking about one-hour detentions, physical labor, or whatever it takes to make students never even want to think about breaking any of your rules.

The truth is, though, that this is really an unrealistic expectation, especially in today's world. All your consequences really have to be is *slightly* annoying. Wow! This is really a great concept. As long as a consequence registers some kind of unpleasantness, even to a small degree, it can be enough to make a student think twice about misbehaving again. Shoot, you can even have a consequence as simple as having students write their name down on a piece of paper. Talk about pain free. There is just something almost magical about a student receiving a consequence that is more tangible than just lip service. Words mean very little. You want your consequences to be concrete.

Now, be sure that you don't confuse these light kinds of consequences with the kind that students should receive for severe misbehavior. If a student curses you out, for instance, you aren't going to just have him or her write a name down on a piece of paper. But smaller consequences can be a great help for those minor infractions that you want to stop but that aren't bad enough to inspire bringing out your most serious punishments.

63. Leave an option open for rules and consequences for unexpected misbehavior.

No matter how hard you try, you can't have a rule for everything. You just may not be able to think of every possible misbehavior that students might dream up. For these situations, it is good to have a general rule of no "uncivilized behavior." That way a student can't claim they shouldn't face a consequence because it wasn't a specific rule being broken. My goal is to have you prepared for anything. The more you are prepared for and the fewer surprises you have, the less stress you will feel.

64. Establish procedures that have no official consequence tied to them.

Every procedure that you have for your students does not have to have a consequence associated with it. Some things should just be done because that is what you expect. The more things that you can handle with just spoken correction, the better off you are. Save official consequences for more serious issues or the times when students refuse to listen to your correction.

65. Be prepared to give a reason for any rule or consequence.

Some students walk in on the first day of school automatically suspicious of teachers. Sometimes for good reason. This is especially true when it comes to the rules that teachers try to establish. Students may think that all teachers make rules just because they like the power. They may wonder why you even have certain rules. Are your rules for their benefit or yours?

There are two good solutions for this dilemma. One, explain to them from day one that all rules are in place to allow students to have the best and safest learning environment possible. And two, always be prepared to give your reason for why you have any rule in place, and be ready to answer this question on the spot. Most students understand the need for rules, and they won't fight one if it makes sense to them. Have a rule that they *don't* think makes sense, though, and you may have conflict.

66. Use direct language about rules and consequences.

Some teachers like things as black and white as possible. Real life is not always so clear cut, of course. When it comes to rules and consequences, though, it will be beneficial for you if you use language that is as clear and straightforward as possible. If you have a classroom rule or if you are asking a student to do something, be sure that you leave no doubt about what you expect.

Avoid general rules like "respect others" without having an explanation of exactly what they mean. One key to having a successful system of rules and consequences is communication. Wishy-washy language will leave you open to criticism as well as potential misunderstandings between you and your students.

67. Don't be too "lecture-y" about consequences.

Sometimes teachers can be tempted to go to their inner parent when students misbehave in the classroom (even if they don't have kids themselves). This is not a good idea. Kids are kids, and although you are in charge of discipline like a parent might be, let's realize your classroom is not quite the same situation.

For example, there may be a time when it is appropriate for a parent to sit down with the child and lecture him or her about the values of right and wrong. Teachers, on the other hand, should be very careful getting into that kind of thing. Getting into lecture mode with students can backfire and ruin your good intentions. Many students will resent you trying to act like their parent. No, there is nothing wrong with teachers talking about manners and good behavior, but it should be presented differently than a parent would. Talk to them matter-of-factly when giving consequences, and don't act in a superior way. Use as few words as possible, get to the point, and move on.

68. Have as many rules as you want.

The skeptics are probably coming out already over this one. Some people in the education world believe strongly that teachers should have absolutely no more than ten rules. Some even may say no more than three. You don't want the students to feel too much stress, after all.

Hogwash. Rules are a part of life. Even if you don't have a formal system of rules and consequences, it is impossible to run a class without rules. There are some very successful teachers who have over fifty. That's right. Fifty. On the other hand, there are also some great teachers who have three rules. The point is to find what works for you. Just be sure that you don't choose so many rules that you can't keep up with all of them or don't really care about enforcing some of them.

Only choose rules that make sense to you and are important to you. And if you think that kids can't handle many rules, ask yourself how many rules there are in football or baseball or other sports that kids play. There haven't been too many students crumbling with stress because of the number of rules in those activities.

69. Don't worry if students say they don't care about your consequence.

This tip is for the specific situation where you are giving one of your consequences and a student says they don't care about it. Chances are, if you teach long enough, this will happen to you at some point. Here is a newsflash: students will test you and your rules. This is no surprise for experienced teachers. One of the ways students may test you is to brazenly tell you that they don't care about your consequences. They may even laugh at you while you give them.

Don't let this get to you. Maybe they do care, and maybe they don't. That is not the point. You have chosen your consequences, and you should stick to them. Whatever you do, don't take away the consequence just because students say it didn't affect them. Make a mental note, yes. But don't cave. It may even be okay to adjust them later if you truly think the consequences aren't effective. Just don't let the student think his or her uprising was the reason you changed the consequence. The student may even be thinking that the consequence was effective but simply not want to admit it.

70. Don't use grades for discipline.

Grades should not be used for discipline. Period. It is true that some teachers are in survival mode and want to use whatever trick they can find to establish order in the classroom. Grades should be the exception, though. Find another way to have consequences for misbehavior, and let the grade strictly reflect the student's knowledge and performance. There is just something about the use of grades for discipline that cheapens their overall evaluation.

71. Don't be afraid to have negatively phrased rules.

Some educators claim that teachers shouldn't phrase rules negatively in any way—that is, having a rule like "*don't* pull someone's hair." (The thinking is that using the word *don't* establishes a bad vibe for the classroom.) This is ridiculous. Enough with this movement to protect students from any possible stress or negativity. Sometimes blunt language is best. Students can handle it.

72. Make reasonable consequences (the law of matching severity).

A lot of teachers seem to think that the key to successful discipline is to have consequences so terrible that students will just be frightened into behaving from the very thought of getting your outrageously bad consequences. While this may be true on some level, the result of having this style of discipline is often disastrous—students will hate and fear you, you will have an extremely stressful teaching experience, and you will find out that you have to keep making your consequences more and more extreme to sustain their effectiveness. Yuck. No thank you.

Instead, make the severity of your consequences match the severity of the misbehavior. For instance, you probably shouldn't send a student to the principal's office for chewing gum. The severity of the consequence is much more severe than the misbehavior. On the other hand, you probably shouldn't just say "please stop" to students who are fighting and do nothing else about it. In that case, the severity of the misbehavior is far greater than the severity of the consequence.

So, the best plan to accomplish matching severities between misbehaviors and consequences is to have a variety of potential consequences that you can go to if needed. Have something on the light end, like a short detention or something even lighter than that (you can even have a consequence of five minutes of no talking for lesser misbehaviors). Come up with a few small consequences that work for you. This will take a little work and thought, but you will be glad you were prepared. Mismatching the severities of consequences and misbehaviors can ruin your classroom management plan fast.

73. Enforce consequences.

This is one of the *fundamentals* to effective discipline, whether you are a teacher, parent, boss, or anyone else in charge. One of the keys to any successful discipline system in the classroom is consistency. Part of that includes following through. The only way that consequences will have any impact at all is if you enforce them when you have said that you will. You absolutely must, must do what you say you are going to do. This includes both negative consequences and positive ones. As soon as you lose the credibility of your word, you are toast. Empty promises or threats will cripple your discipline credibility faster than you can say "I said stop it."

74. Display your rules and consequences prominently (even if they are informal).

Having your rules and consequences displayed will accomplish two things for you: first, you will make it easier for students to remember them, and second, your students will not be able to have the "out" of being able to say that you never told them about that rule or that they forgot it. The second one may sound a little cynical, but it is best to be prepared for the "sneaky" student.

75. Don't let students huddle at the door.

This one is very specific for sure. There is just something that seems out of control when students huddle at the door before the bell rings or at the end of class. Something about groups of students in close proximity seems to lend itself to mischief. Be proactive and have them sit until it's time to go. Guard against easy opportunities for students to misbehave and you will be better off than trying to put out little fires all day.

76. Eliminate the phrase "shut up."

There is just something powerfully negative about the phrase "shut up." It is hard to understand why this is even true. There is no doubt, though, that people have fought and probably done worse just over being told to shut up. Even telling someone to shut up in a joking way can cause tension. So do yourself a favor and forbid the use of this ugly phrase in your classroom. And yes, this includes you, the teacher, too.

77. Don't insist on around-the-clock quiet.

The noise level in a class is often associated with the amount of "control" a teacher has. This is not necessarily the case. Sometimes great learning can occur even in what seems to be chaos. The real test of a teacher's classroom management ability is the level of cooperation that students give. Being quiet or loud has nothing to do with it. If the teacher is allowing, or even encouraging, students to be loud, then there should be no criticism of that teacher. So the next time you walk past or evaluate a noisy class, don't automatically assume the teacher has lost them. It might be exactly what he or she has allowed.

78. Don't allow students to argue excessively.

Students learn a lot of content in school, but life skills are important as well. One of those skills is knowing how to handle a situation where you disagree with someone. Students may not know any better, or they may be used to handling disagreements with yelling, screaming, disrespecting, and so on. Teach them that it is okay to disagree sometimes, but it is not okay to handle the disagreement poorly. Teach them good lessons about disagreeing and you will have a much happier and more peaceful classroom. You may even give your students a good lesson to teach their parents too.

79. Don't tolerate meanness or disrespect among students.

Kids can be mean. This is nothing new. So keep your ears open to see if someone may be getting picked on or bullied. Even if it seems like it is being done in fun, the student being insulted may not think so. Sometimes you may be the only one who will stand up for a student, and your classroom may be the only safe place he or she has at school.

80. Don't allow any signs of racism.

This should go without saying, of course. Be alert, though, for even a hint of casual use of racist language, and put a fast stop to it. Stopping it early can save you the drama of having it get more serious later.

81. Don't allow excessive complaining.

Let's face it, sometimes kids can be a little bratty. They may whine and complain when they don't get their way, or they may even throw temper tantrums. This doesn't mean they are bad kids. It may mean that they have never been taught that this kind of behavior won't actually work. You may be the lucky one who gets to teach them this lesson. If you do find yourself in the presence of an excessive whiner or complainer, the best thing to do is shut that behavior down quickly.

Let the complaining student know that this won't be tolerated. Tell them something like, "I won't talk to you until you talk to me in a calm voice," or even give a more serious consequence if the behavior continues. By the time a student is a teenager, if he or she is still a brat, the student has never been taught this lesson. You will do the world a favor if you contribute to making one less brat out there.

Chapter Two

Mental Health

Teachers sometimes get a reputation for being superheroes, but they can have their issues just like anyone else. Teaching can be a very difficult, stressful occupation. Teachers face the stresses of everything from stage fright to test-score pressure to parent harassment. Teachers who want to keep their sanity should be proactively doing things to protect their mental stability.

82. Don't eat lunch alone.

Everyone has heard of the studies saying that eating alone is bad for your health. This may be even truer for teachers. Teaching can be a stressful job; it is good to mingle with other adults instead of just being around kids all day. So try to avoid the habit of eating alone in your room and find some coworkers to eat with—and try not to talk about work all the time!

83. Live at least fifteen minutes away from where you teach.

The 24/7 teacher life can burn you out in a hurry. When you live in the same city where you teach, or even close to it, your job can follow you. You will run into parents and students in the grocery store, at the dentist, and wherever else you go. Even when you don't actually come in contact with people that you know from school, there can be other people who *know people* from school who are watching your every move. This may sound a little paranoid, but it is actually not too far away from the reality these days. This is not to say that you have anything to hide. There is something a little odd to me about being under the microscope that comes with a teaching job. Teachers are almost like a kind of mini celebrity in their area. This is not a situation you want to be in, if given a choice.

If you are not concerned about these types of scenarios, then there is no reason to follow this advice. Feel free to live in the closet in your classroom if you want. There is just something nice about the thought of being able to get away from life at school and not have to be in "teacher mode" all the time. If you agree, do yourself a favor and protect your mental health by putting a little distance between you and your school. Teaching is a noble, honorable career. There is no reason that it has to be your *entire* life, though.

84. Don't overdo your workload.

Teachers sometimes seem to get a guilt trip if they aren't working around the clock. They feel like they are failing their students if they aren't squeezing out every moment of attention and effort for them. This is not healthy. There is a point where your workload becomes too much to handle. An excessive workload can lead to lower performance, stress, and burnout. This is a dangerous mental place to be. You won't be doing anyone any good if you aren't able to teach anymore. So watch that workload. Learn to say no to some of your extra activities. The students need you!

85. Slow down when you get nervous.

Some may be surprised to hear that teachers may need advice about overcoming nerves. Teachers are superheroes, right? Some teachers may make it look like they are indestructible and perfect, but they are far from it. Some can even get a case of stage fright or social anxiety.

There are teachers who speak with complete ease and comfort in the classroom but fall apart at the thought of talking in a school assembly or even at a faculty meeting. Public-speaking skills are not just a blanket talent that people either have or don't have. You may be great in one speaking situation but terrible in another. Or you may be totally fine speaking one day and then nervous the next day in the exact *same* situation. It is strange how the mind can work sometimes.

One of the most important rules of successful public speaking is to do whatever it takes to find your comfort zone. The method of finding this happy place may be drastically different for different people. There is no one magic answer that will solve all of your public-speaking weaknesses. In general, the best thing you can do when you get nervous is to slow down. Take a few deep breaths. Talk a little more slowly. And focus on the positive. Public-speaking difficulties can be overcome. The trick is finding what works best for you.

86. Don't be obsessed with the calendar.

Everyone loves weekends, holidays, and other kinds of time off. There is nothing wrong with that. It is probably true that you will hear comments about it almost being Friday, five o'clock, and so on around most places. There is nothing wrong with appreciating your breaks. Just don't let yourself become *obsessed* with them. If you hate your job so much that you live for the times when you don't have to go to work, it may be time to find a new profession. Also, spending your whole life hanging on for whatever break is coming up in the future is a good way to let your life move right past you. Appreciate where you are in the moment. Enjoy your breaks when they happen. Just don't let your entire happiness depend on them.

87. Don't be too proud to ask for help from other teachers.

Teachers can sometimes be intimidating, even to other teachers. You may feel uncomfortable or even embarrassed to ask other teachers for help if you are having trouble with something. This is a mistake. Yes, there are some cranky teachers out there who selfishly want to keep all of their ideas to themselves and who will not help you. These kinds of teachers are rare exceptions, though. Most are willing and eager to help and maybe even to show off their knowledge a little. Your fellow teachers can be an extremely valuable resource for you when things get tough. Be sure you take advantage of the opportunity.

88. Make time to have a social life (especially if you are single).

Teaching is definitely not the only stressful career in existence, but there is something about it that seems to drain people on a different level. Maybe it is the mental side of it. Maybe it is the need to pay attention to your surroundings every second of every day. Who knows. Whatever the cause, it seems like teachers often have a tougher time having a social life than people in other careers.

It can be very tempting just to veg out when you get home after a long day in the classroom. You may not be in the mood to see or talk to anybody. As a result, your life becomes a never-ending cycle of teaching, going home, recovering, preparing for the next school day, and then starting all over again. Ugh. Continue this cycle year after year and you will look up and wonder where the school year went.

Don't let yourself fall into this teach-and-recover cycle. Get out and socialize every now and then, even if you have to force yourself sometimes. Make an effort to have a life outside of teaching and your teaching life and performance will probably be better too.

89. Don't depend on approval from the boss.

Some teachers say that they want to leave their job because they don't get enough pats on the back from their boss. Yikes. You have the wrong mind-set if this is the way you think. Teachers should be focused on one thing and one thing only—serving and doing what is best for students. If your administrators notice you doing that and give you praise, great! But you shouldn't need that kind of motivation. Think of approval as a luxury, not a requirement. Remember why you do what you do. Hopefully, administrator approval is way down on the list, if it is even there at all.

90. Count your blessings.

It is hard to understand how some teachers can be constant gripers. "I hate this, I hate that," they say. It seems like everything that comes out of their mouths is a complaint of some kind. Everyone has troubles, but there are some teachers who could use a little attitude adjustment. Do you know how much you have going for you compared to most of the rest of the world? Do you know how grateful you should be that you even have a job? If you hate your job that much, do yourself and your students a favor and find a new career. Either that or look for a new place to work. This constant moaning about everything you don't like is not good for you or the people around you. Okay, my preaching is over. Now on to lighter topics.

91. Avoid doing school-related summer jobs.

Protecting your mental health is important if you want to be a successful educator. Many teachers don't pay enough attention to this. Some teachers need to make extra money, and teaching summer school may pay the most. That is hard to argue with. If you have a long-term goal of teaching for a while, though, it is probably not a good idea. Sacrifice the short-term payoff for the long-term benefit of staying fresh for the upcoming school year.

92. Get up early the last few days of vacation.

This tip may bring an avalanche of hate mail, but it is an important one. Abrupt changes to sleeping patterns can make it painful to try to adjust. Be smart and start getting on schedule for waking up early a couple of days before you go back to school so you don't have such a shock the first day back. You will be glad you did.

93. Save at least one weekend day as a day for zero schoolwork.

If you notice, there are multiple tips about giving yourself mental breaks from teaching. Taking breaks should be viewed not as a sign of weakness but rather as wise long-term planning. Making your teaching career an around-the-clock endeavor is such a terrible idea. This point needs to be stressed. If you have a lot of work to do at home, try to do it all by Saturday. Or skip Saturday if you want and do it Sunday. Whatever you do, try to pick one day when you can take a break from thinking about teaching and protect that mental health!

94. Tough it out if you are teaching and taking classes of your own on the side.

Sometimes an extra degree or certification can be a big help for your teaching skills and/or finances. It is usually worth it if you can manage the time, but it can be *very* difficult. You may have to drive a long way to get to your classes after a stressful day of teaching. You will have homework that will have to be done after you have finished all of your grading and planning. If you want it badly enough, though, you can pull it off. Just keep your nose to the grindstone and tough it out until you finish the program. You can do it.

95. Know how to handle days when you come to school in a bad mood.

Everyone has had days when you knew you were in a bad mood before the day even started. Maybe you had an argument with a spouse that morning. Maybe you didn't sleep well. Whatever the cause, there will inevitably be days that will get off to a bad start.

When you know ahead of time that you are feeling a little cranky, instead of just writing the day off as a loss, try to overcome whatever has caused your bad mood. It can be done. Maybe you have to take a few deep breaths. Maybe you will need a little self–pep talk. Do whatever works for you. There is something powerful about being self-aware. Use it to your advantage. Get yourself into a better frame of mind when you know things aren't so good for reasons that have nothing to do with school. Your students will be the ones who benefit the most.

96. Don't give students power over your emotions.

Keeping your emotions under control in the classroom can be a challenge. Students know this. Some students can really push your buttons, and they enjoy having that little bit of power over you. Don't let them. It may take a little will power, but staying under control when students are trying to get a rise out of you is tremendously powerful. You will be much better off if you handle discipline issues like you are an unemotional scorekeeper (see tip #3). Deprive students of the thrill of getting you flustered or upset, and a lot of the fun of their misbehavior will disappear.

97. Don't hate your job.

If you hate your job in education, it is probably time to do something else. You don't necessarily have to be dancing out of bed every day looking forward to it, but if you dread going, you aren't doing anybody any good. If you truly hate what you are doing, get out as fast as you can. Ride out the school year if you don't feel good about leaving in the middle, but find something else to do. Life is too short to have a job you hate, no matter how worthy the cause.

98. Take as little schoolwork home as possible.

The 24/7 teacher never makes it in the long run. If you want your career as a teacher to last, you should do whatever you can to avoid the teacher-workaholic lifestyle. One of the factors that contributes to the overworked teacher life is the amount of schoolwork that you do away from school.

Make your best effort to eliminate, or at least minimize, what you take home with you. Stay and work late if you have to, but the less you do at home, the better your state of mind will be. Being able to have some free home time without schoolwork hanging over you is a nice feeling, even if it's for a small amount of time.

Some of you may not have a choice. You may have kids or some other reason that prevents you from staying late at school. If that is the case, you may not be able to completely eliminate working at home. In these situations, do what you can to at least *minimize* what you have to do at home. Use your time efficiently when you are at school, and take as little home as possible.

99. Take things one day at a time.

A tough teaching situation can be overwhelming sometimes. If you are feeling overwhelmed by student misbehavior, your workload, or just teaching in general, remember that all you have to do is deal with tomorrow. Try not to think about how many days you have ahead of you or how difficult they might be. Take care of tomorrow, then the next day. Before you know it, you will be through with the tough season that felt like would last forever.

100. Don't take on extra duties if you have a choice.

Saying no can be tough, especially if you are new to a school. You want to look like a team player. Your number one priority should be your teaching duties, however. Don't let extra duties take away from your performance in the classroom. If the boss insists that you do something, accept it. There is nothing you can do about that. But don't volunteer for extra work just to try to look good. Protect your teaching performance however you can!

101. Savor your summer break.

The vacation time that most teachers get is one of the big perks of the job. It can be easy to get used to your long breaks a few days or weeks into them, but be sure you aren't taking this time for granted when you get it. Most people don't get that kind of time off.

102. Keep an eye on long-term plans.

One of the dangers that teachers face is the temptation to get caught up in daily routines. Don't let this happen to you. Always know what your long-term goals are, and make sure that everything you do fits into those plans. Have your semester/year planned out, at least with a general overview. Living and planning one day at a time will wear you out.

103. Go to church, meditate, do yoga, or whatever you do to relax.

Are there enough tips about the importance of taking care of your mental and emotional health? However many there are, there are still not enough. Be sure that you find some way to relax outside of school. If you don't have something that you do already, keep trying things until you find what works for you. This can't be stressed enough.

104. Have friends outside of school.

Have you ever noticed how students' entire worlds often seem to revolve around what is going on at school? All of their friends are there. The person they date is there. All of their social events take place there. And on and on.

It does not have to be this way for teachers. Don't let your entire life be wrapped up in what happens at school. Have friends and activities that you enjoy that have no connection to your school. There is nothing wrong with having school spirt and being into your students and their lives. Just don't let it *consume* you.

We all know teachers who seem to have their entire lives wrapped up in school. All of their friends are teachers. All they talk about is what is going on at school. They are completely obsessed with school. Try not to let this happen to you.

105. Don't let a few jerky students steal your joy of teaching.

Would it be a shocking statement to say that there is a percentage of the population who are just jerks? It is probably not a large percentage—it seems that in general most people are good. But there is definitely a population of jerks out there (and criminals too if we are being honest).

Since this is the case, that means that there is also a percentage of students who are just not nice people. Some of them may even show up in your classroom. Be prepared for them. Don't let these not-so-nice people ruin your teaching experience. Now, don't mistake this advice to mean that you should somehow shun this group of bad characters or treat them poorly in some way. Just don't answer jerky behavior with similar behavior of your own. It is still your job to teach these students and give them the best education possible. Just don't give them the power to ruin your day.

106. Underreact instead of overreact to stressful situations.

Easier said than done, right? Most things are not as big a deal as they seem in the moment. Make it your goal to underreact instead of overreact during times of stress and you will find yourself feeling a lot better about the way you handle things.

107. Keep your self-respect.

When the day is over, one of your goals in the classroom should be always to try to feel good about the way you handled yourself. Were you mean to students? Did you lose your cool? Did you act in a way that would embarrass you if anyone found out about it? This goal will give you clarity. When the day is over, you can look back and ask yourself if you accomplished it. If you didn't, you can learn from your mistake and try to correct it for the future.

108. Don't let yourself fall into the mind-set of just "surviving" days.

Have you ever asked someone how they were doing and their answer was "just surviving"? Don't let yourself think that way. No matter how bad your days might be, you still have a lot going for you. Focus on the positive, and try to make the best of your situation. No matter how bad your situation might be, you are still helping kids.

109. Have a servant mind-set.

Anytime you mention the word *servant* people can get a little uncomfortable. But this word can have a positive association when applied to teachers—at least the ones who want to do the job right. Your job is to serve students. It's as simple as that. You may be the authority figure, and you may be in charge, but you are still there to serve. Thinking about just surviving puts all of your focus on you. Flip that around and focus on what you can do for students; you will have a much more fulfilling and productive experience.

110. Have a go-to verse or motivational quote memorized to go to when things get tough.

Let's face it, teaching can sometimes be outrageous. If you have taught long enough, you have probably dealt with some wild situations along the way. And it doesn't matter where you teach, what grade you teach, what level you teach, or whatever. There is always the potential for craziness. So be prepared.

This tip may sound a little gimmicky, but it is always a good idea to do whatever it takes to keep your emotions and stress levels in check. There may be times during your teaching career when you feel like you just can't take it anymore, not even one more minute. You feel like you are just going to lose it. Hopefully, you will never have this happen to you, but if you ever can see yourself feeling this way in class, you might want to have a motivational verse or quote to go to. Just a little self–pep talk to get yourself into the right frame of mind.

111. Don't go on and on talking to friends and family about school issues.

It seems like for some teachers, school is their entire life, and their entire world revolves around what happens at school. But guess what—your friends and family don't want to hear about it. There may be an exception to this if you have a really interesting story to tell, but don't be the teacher who talks about every little thing that is going on at school. Stop giving teachers a bad name by making them all look like constant complainers and gossipers.

112. Know how to be at your best during official observations.

Most schools these days have some kind of observation process for teachers. The observation will either be for an entire period or a portion of one. These evaluations scare some teachers to *death*. It doesn't matter how long they have been teaching or how many awards they have won, there is just something about being observed that makes them cringe.

The answer for most teachers is simply to figure out a way to be your usual self when the observation occurs. You are good, and you know you are good. You just want to show it.

One technique that can help you get to your usual comfort zone is to think of observers as members of your class. Even administrators/observers are just guests in your classroom. It is your domain. Think of them like any other student in there and you will be able to continue with business as usual.

113. Include the observers in your class discussions during official observations.

There is no need to walk on eggshells and pretend that observers and evaluators aren't even in the room. Include them in your discussions and you will break the tension of them being there. This trick can do wonders for your comfort level during those stressful times when you are observed. Just be sure that you don't take it *too* far and include administrators so much that you neglect your students!

114. Don't kiss up to the observers during official observations.

Yes, you want to make your best effort when you are being observed, but let's make an effort to avoid trying too hard and kissing up to them. Most people can see right through that anyway. Just try your best and do your usual teaching magic and let the chips fall where they may.

115. Ask students ahead of time to be on their best behavior when you know an observation is coming.

There is nothing wrong with telling students ahead of time that you will be observed. If they like you, they will probably try to be on their best behavior for you. Even if they don't like you, they may act better knowing that they are being watched too. You probably shouldn't make your request for good behavior sound like a threat of some kind; simply make it clear that everyone will probably be better off if the observation goes well.

Story Time: After studying discipline for the first couple of years of my teaching career, I began to gain some confidence in my skills in this area. One time, during my first year at a school, I decided I would show off a little. So, when I heard that I would be observed during a particularly rowdy class, I told the students to act how they normally would during the observation. I instructed them to pretend like the observer (principal) was not even there. The idea was that the observer would see these students behaving poorly and I would display my tremendous classroom management skills. Big mistake.

Just as they had been instructed, the class acted in the same rowdy way they always had, maybe even more than usual. As a result, I had a very unfavorable observation. If I had not received high marks on my other three observations that year, things might have gotten ugly for me. So, don't play with fire, my friends. If you know an observation is coming, always ask your class to behave well for you.

116. Don't be a victim.

You may not be able to control what happens to you at school during your teaching day, but you can control your responses. Let's face it, you do not know what is going to happen on any given day at school. Your students may behave like ladies and gentlemen, or you may have pandemonium. Or you may have anything in between. If and when the bad times do happen, don't be a victim or get a "woe is me" attitude. You can find the positive in just about any situation, even if that positive is learning that teaching is not the career for you!

117. Get up early enough not to have to rush.

There is no denying that sleep is a hugely valuable asset for teachers. No doubt about it. But the stress of having to rush in the morning probably won't be worth getting a few minutes of extra sleep. Even waking up five or ten minutes earlier can make a huge difference in reducing the amount of rushing (and therefore stress) that you have to deal with.

118. Don't fear embarrassment in class.

There are teachers who daily live in fear of being embarrassed in front of their students. "What if I make a mistake? What if I do something dumb? What if I pass gas?" and on and on. If you want to make it in the long run as a teacher and keep your mental health intact, you absolutely must get over the fear of embarrassment. What is the worst thing that can happen to you? Your students laugh at you?

Don't fear embarrassment. Prepare yourself to show your students how little things don't bother you and you will have a lot more peace of mind.

119. Don't make yourself available *every* day before and after school.

Yes, it is great to be willing to take time to help your students outside of class. You should probably do this a lot, if needed. Just don't feel like you are obligated to be there for students *all* the time. It is okay to set an availability schedule and only meet with students during those times. You still need to save time for planning, grading papers, and so on. Don't let a guilty feeling of having to help students on demand stop you from your other duties as a teacher.

120. Know ahead of time what circumstance is bad enough to make you quit.

What it would take to make you quit your job is a bit of an unpleasant topic, but the reality is that there should be some things that would make you leave. Know what those things are ahead of time so you don't react in the moment.

Maybe administrative grade changing behind your back is on your list. Maybe excessive violence at your school would make you consider leaving. Maybe you have something completely different that would bring you to such an extreme reaction. Whatever the case is for you, realize that there may be some situations that would be serious enough to make you consider quitting or at least changing schools. Make sure you know what would be on your list.

121. Save kind notes from students.

If you teach long enough, you will probably get a kind note, Christmas card, goodbye gift, or another small token from a student every now and then. Save them. They can be a good boost of positive energy during tough times or when your career is over and you want to reminisce.

122. Be content.

Sometimes it is better to try to focus on the positive. Be glad you have a job. There are plenty of people who don't. Be glad you are doing something that will have a positive impact on people (if you are doing it right). This obviously can be easier said than done, but it is important to be content and thankful for the good things about your teaching career instead of focusing on the negative. A positive mind-set can have a huge impact on your mental health, productivity, and overall view of your teaching career.

123. Have an "oh well" attitude about something not going right.

One of the worst mistakes that teachers make is to make mountains out of molehills. The reality is that most bad things that happen aren't *that* big of a deal. Even the worst-behaving kid is usually not going to do anything that will cause you permanent harm. Try to let things roll off your back. If things are really bad, you may have to have a "press on" kind of attitude, but even then you should be able to brush off most bad days. The sun will come again the next day, and you will have a chance to reset and change things for the better.

124. Don't worry about "what ifs" of student behavior, test scores, and so on.

The easiest way to cause yourself stress is to worry about things that are out of your control. The number one fear for teachers may very well be that students will misbehave in some way and they won't know how to handle it (with low test scores being a close second).

If you are worried about discipline, you might want to try developing a more formal discipline plan for your classes—one where you know exactly what you will do to handle any situation. Eliminate the worry of uncertainty by being as organized as possible about how you will handle certain misbehaviors. If you are worried about low test scores, all you can really do is do your best and see what happens. There is no good that can come from worrying about it.

125. Have a few "self-talk" phrases to go to when things get tough.

Teaching can be stressful. If you teach long enough, there will be times when you may be stressed, anxious, or even out of control. There are a variety of things that can throw you off your game: misbehaving students, an argument at home, conflict with the boss. Whatever.

When (not if) trouble occurs, it is a good idea to be prepared ahead of time for these situations. Some psychologists believe in the idea of "self-talk" to get yourself through anxious moments. This is not some complicated and deep idea. It simply means that you have a phrase or two to repeat to yourself during tense moments.

A lot of athletes use this strategy. If you are a religious person, you might want to have a Bible verse ready. Or you may just want to have a simple phrase like "stay calm" or "keep your composure" that you can go to. Use whatever works for you, and figure it out before you get into those kinds of situations. When the going gets tough, it is much better to be proactive rather than reactive.

126. Don't let students mess with you.

Students can sometimes be mean, even to teachers. You can't let this kind of behavior affect you. If a student teases you in some way, let it roll off your back. Whether or not you discipline him or her is not the point here. Make it your goal to let go of those jerky kinds of student comments. The best way to accomplish this mind-set is not to care too much about being liked.

127. Know that the year will come to an end at some point.

If you are having a rough school year or if you have a particularly difficult class, sometimes it can seem like it will go on forever. The longer you teach, the more you realize just how fast the school year can go by. So if you feel like your challenging class is going to drive you crazy forever, realize that the school year will end at some point. A change in perspective can really help improve your outlook.

Chapter Three

Wellness

Most teachers are dedicated to their job and their students, otherwise they wouldn't be in the profession. Being too dedicated can be dangerous, though. Workaholism can easily cause ineffectiveness, physical and mental issues, and burnout. The teacher who wants to stay in the profession for the long run should be careful to take care of themselves along the way. A burned-out teacher is no good to anyone.

128. Be generally healthy.

Teaching is a stressful job. There is no getting around this fact, no matter how good or experienced you are. Be wise and take care of your health so teaching doesn't have a negative effect on your well-being. Eating, exercising, and sleeping right will also do a lot to help your mind-set and ability to keep your cool when things get tough.

129. Don't use vending machines at school.

Ugh. These things are mostly bad for your health, not to mention bad for your pocketbook. Enough said.

130. Don't come to school sick.

Yes, your schedule may be tight, and you may have no time to spend on your long-term substitute plans, but don't feel like you have to be a superhero and come to school sick. Stay home, rest up, and don't get people at school sick. Your performance will probably be better in the long run too.

131. Try to get at least seven hours of sleep.

Teachers are notoriously sleep deprived. Some seem to think that it just goes with the job. This does not have to be true. This may be an ambitious goal, but try to average around seven hours or more of sleep if you can. There seems to be a big connection between sleep and good physical and mental health. Make it a priority.

132. Bring your own lunch.

School lunches can be expensive over the long run, not to mention often unhealthy. Do your health and your pocketbook a favor and pack a lunch as much as possible.

133. Avoid soda.

The caffeine and sugar (or worse, artificial sweetener) combination is literally poison. If you are making it a priority to watch your health so you can teach better and live longer, then soda needs to be high on the list of things to cut out or at least drastically reduce.

134. Don't stay up too late on the weekends.

Unfortunately, most jobs in education don't allow for the luxury of sleeping in very often. Many of them require you to get up at 6 a.m. or earlier. Don't try to beat the system by staying up extremely late on the weekends, then drastically changing your sleeping habits during the week. Big swings are not good for you, especially as you get older. Your students deserve you at your best. Keep that sleeping schedule somewhat consistent.

135. Have some snacks stashed for the afternoon.

If you are a caring teacher at all, you will likely find yourself staying later than normal hours often. Be prepared and have some snacks stashed in your room for these situations. If you don't, you will likely either cave and go to the snack machine or you will not have the energy to get much work done. And, of course, you are more likely to binge on junk food when you get home, which is never good.

136. Walk/exercise just before school or just after school if you can.

Handling stress is a very important part of being an educator. It doesn't matter how good you are at discipline and classroom management or how positive a person you are, your teaching job will inevitably give you a lot of stress. Make a commitment to exercise on a daily basis if you can. Right before you leave for school or right after you leave is best. Thirty to forty-five minutes is all you need to start chasing some of that stress and tension away.

137. Cook enough food for more than one meal at a time.

Efficiency seems to be an overlooked quality in education these days. The reality is that you just don't have enough minutes in the day to be wasting many. The effort you make cooking can be a major time drain. Cook enough food for an extra meal or two and save some precious minutes during your day.

138. Don't overdo fast food.

Convenience isn't a good enough reason to sacrifice health. Plan your meals, even when you don't feel like doing it. There is just something about too much fast food that makes you feel blah.

139. Drink water throughout the day.

Drinking water keeps you hydrated, which can improve your health, improve your thinking, and keep you more alert. Not bad for something you can get for free.

140. Don't look at your phone right before bed.

They say that looking at the kind of bright light that comes out of your TV or phone can mess up your sleep cycle. That should be enough to consider closing up both a half hour or so before hitting the sack.

141. Don't sit all day.

Sitting too much will make you gain weight and cause sluggishness. If your class is taking a test or you know you will be sitting for long periods of time, remind yourself to get up and walk around every thirty minutes or so. This is especially important if you supervise a class where the students are working at a computer for most of the time. Don't let yourself stay seated all day every day. You will pay a price.

142. Join a gym.

Exercise does three things that are major benefits for teachers: it improves your health and resistance to sickness, it reduces stress, and it helps your brain power. Sounds good!

143. Don't skip lunch.

Yes, you have work to do. Yes, time is scarce. But you shouldn't make a habit of skipping lunch. Get that fuel you need for the rest of the day. And, of course, don't take shortcuts by getting something unhealthy from the snack machine.

144. Eat breakfast.

Being hungry can make you cranky and think less clearly. Wake up a few minutes early if that is what it takes. Don't underestimate the benefits of eating breakfast.

145. Take naps if possible.

Time is scarce for teachers. Even just thirty minutes of napping can be a huge benefit, though. Plan your day so that you can get one or two naps in per week and you will feel much better and fresher in the long run.

146. Splurge on a good mattress, pillows, and so on.

Value that sleep! It can literally be the difference between success and failure. And if you really want to go for as much comfort as possible, investing in a good pair of comfortable shoes can't hurt either.

Chapter Four

Success

Everyone wants to be successful. Success for teachers can include everything from high test scores to great relationships to a general sense of doing good. There are no easy tricks to getting there, but there are some things that teachers can do to help their chances.

147. Don't believe everything your college professors told you.

College professors can be very helpful. Some of yours may have even inspired you to become a teacher. Many of them may not been in the classroom for years—if at all—when you took their course. Always take what they say with a grain of salt. People with actual, recent experience in the classroom can often teach you things that your professors could not.

148. Finish the year strong.

It is very easy for both students and teachers alike to see the end of the school year coming and start to coast a little. It's a natural reaction. As the adult and leader of your classes, however, it is very important that you stay mentally tough and finish strong. Don't slack off just because you see summer vacation coming around the corner. Be a good example for your students of what it looks like to stay focused all year long.

149. Don't take days off that you don't really need.

You are paid to do a job. It is probably not the most honorable thing in the world to take days off when you really aren't sick. It is hard to argue against the benefits of a "mental health day" every now and then, but there is just something that feels wrong about doing that—especially with the massive amounts of days off that teachers get anyway. If teaching is stressing you out so much that you are not mentally able to go to work when you are supposed to, you may want to think about doing something else. Teaching is very difficult, but your students pay the price when you aren't there. Stay true to your commitment to them, and don't be frivolous about the time you take off.

150. Have enthusiasm for your subject and for teaching—even if you have to fake it.

Let's face it, you are probably not going to be pumped up and excited to teach *every* single day of the school year. That is normal. But your students still deserve your best. Try to give your students that every day, even if you have to fake some energy every now and then.

151. Try to teach in your strengths.

All teachers have strengths and weaknesses. If you want to be at your best, try to have some self-awareness about the grades, subjects, and so forth that best fit your skills and personality and try to get a job where you are working in those strengths. Hit your teaching sweet spot and your teaching will be much more successful and enjoyable.

You obviously may not always have control over your teaching schedule. Sometimes you just have to do what you are told. If you have any choice in the matter, though, be ready to know where you can be most useful.

152. Overplan your lessons.

One of the biggest causes of stress for teachers is lack of preparation. Fortunately, this problem is easy to fix. If you often feel the stress of having to think on the fly during class or if you find yourself finishing too early and leaving idle time at the end of the period, then you should increase your planning efforts. You might even want to plan for *more* than the time you have allotted in class. Leave no doubt that you will have plenty of work for your students to do during their time with you and have every minute planned.

153. Have emergency plans ready.

You never know when you might miss work unexpectedly or even have a day when you aren't thinking straight because of a traumatic event in your life. These things happen. Be prepared for those times when you just won't be able to have your normal day in class.

154. Do your homework about a school before accepting a job.

Some administrators can get desperate when the beginning of a school year is approaching and they still have teaching jobs to fill. They may even be tempted to stretch the truth a little about student behavior, your role at the school, coaching, and so on in an effort to lure you over. It is impossible to know exactly what a school will be like before you start working there, but be wise and do a little research to know what you are getting into. Try to talk to teachers who work there if you can. The more you know, the better your chances are of making an informed decision.

155. Try not to have substitute teachers giving tests.

It is just too hard to police cheating, no matter how much you trust the sub. Play it safe and if possible postpone your tests when you have to miss a day of school.

156. Teach more than just your subject. Teach life skills.

Content is not the only thing students can learn from you. You have a lot more to offer than that. You can teach social skills, manners, and so on as well. Make it your goal to make your students better off for having had your class—both in general knowledge and in life skills.

157. Don't write off Fridays.

Don't be one of those teachers who decides that Friday is a good day to take off and just throw in a movie or full-period video. Your students have a limited amount of time with you. Make it your goal to waste as little of it as possible.

158. Don't cut corners out of fear of failing students.

Grade worship. Ugh. It's a growing trend in education. There is so much pressure on teachers to give students passing grades that it is easy to see why they might be tempted to dumb things down a little just to make sure everyone has an acceptable grade. Or worse yet, "give" grades that students don't deserve. Do not let this pressure affect your integrity as a teacher. The intent of most grade pressure is good—to motivate teachers to do the best they can to help their students pass. Unfortunately, the result of this pressure is often not more effort but an attempt to find more ways to beat the system.

159. Help students by having them practice public speaking.

One of the most common questions that students will ever ask is "Why do we need this?" A lot of times the question may be hard for teachers to answer. Public speaking, though, is not in this category. Public-speaking skills and comfort is one of the most valuable things that students can learn in school.

Most jobs require some kind of speaking or interpersonal interaction with others. Require as much public speaking as you can in your class, no matter the subject matter. And don't listen to people who might tell you not to require students to do public speaking because it could stress them out. Learning to deal with the stresses of public speaking and communication is a great lesson to learn at any age.

160. Help students' social skills by giving group work.

Group work used to be one of the hot trends in education. While this type of assignment's popularity has slowed somewhat, it is still not without benefits. This is not to suggest that you structure your entire class based on group work or even that you do it every week. Just try to work in into your routine occasionally. People skills are extremely useful for students, whether it is for their future careers or even just their success in high school. As a civilized society, the ability to work with people who are different than you, disagree with you, or challenge you in some way is key to making it.

161. Don't protect students from failure.

A lot of well-intentioned teachers and parents try to protect their kids from any possible negative experience. Failure and disappointment are seen as the enemy. The logic is hard to debate, but learning how to deal with failure and tough times is a valuable skill for students. Most successful people did not just become instantly successful—it likely took work and overcoming failure along the way. If you try to protect your students from every bad thing that might happen to them, the result is that you are going to make them weak. So give them a chance to fail. Don't go messing with their failing grades or telling them something is okay when it's not. Your students will benefit a lot more from truthful language then sugarcoating.

162. Bring your best effort every day—even if you don't feel like it.

Most teachers have 90 to 180 days or so with their students. That is a lot of days to have to be "on" during a given year. Let's face it, you won't always feel enthused to teach. No matter how you feel, however, it is still important to bring your best effort. Your students deserve it. Think of yourself like a performer onstage. Even if you are a little sick, unenthusiastic, or not feeling up to the task, the show must go on.

163. Don't become a teacher for the days off.

Some people actually consider getting into a career in education for all of the great vacation time you get. Ha! Yes, the vacation time is definitely a perk for teachers. But you still have to work for about forty weeks a year. That sounds great, but if you aren't cut out for it, those forty weeks could become a living hell.

164. Video yourself teaching.

Sometimes another perspective can help you see things that you otherwise wouldn't. You might be amazed to see what you actually look like, from the students' side of things, when you are teaching. So if your goal is truly to be as good as you can possibly be, you might want to consider videoing yourself. You may get some insight that you wouldn't get otherwise.

165. Don't automatically follow the latest trends.

Stay in education long enough and you will see a regular stream of the new latest and greatest fad that is going to transform education. Sometimes they last and have a positive effect, sometimes they fade away like the fad they are. New math! Open classrooms! Block scheduling! No homework! Remember those things?

Some innovations are better than others. At some point, people thought that their new thing was the great idea that was going to save education. That label has been assigned to many "great" ideas over the years and decades that have simply fallen flat. So use your common sense and don't be afraid to disagree with the crowd.

166. Embrace technology.

It's the twenty-first century. Deal with it. Don't let yourself be the old guy who hates progress and refuses to change with the times.

167. Give back.

There are so many wise teachers out there. Even the ones who aren't so great overall probably have a good idea or two. So don't hide whatever wisdom you have. Go public. Get on social media. Talk shop with your coworkers. Educators are all in this together!

168. Don't be shy about asking coworkers about their success methods.

Teachers have a wealth of knowledge. Don't miss out on it because of shyness or fear of getting told no! Step it up, ask for help, and improve your skills.

169. Read books, blogs, professional magazines, and so on about teaching-success methods.

If you want to improve your teaching skills, take advantage of other teachers' wisdom. It's everywhere.

170. Find ways to improve your public-speaking skills outside of school.

Public speaking is an important part of successful teaching. If you aren't a total public-speaking master, it might be a good idea to find other ways practice it whenever you can. Join Toastmasters. Call in to your local radio talk show. Sing some karaoke. Get creative with it. Do whatever it takes to make yourself an even better speaker than you already are.

171. Plan every day as if you are going to be observed.

Sometimes it can be easy to get a little comfortable within the walls of your own classroom. You may feel like you are in your own little world. But don't let that comfort cause you to get sloppy. Plan every day like you want to make a great impression for an observation. This mind-set will elevate your performance, and it you will also be prepared for those days an administrator actually does pop in.

172. Decorate your classroom.

The way you have your room set up can affect the vibe your students feel. Is it a positive place? Is it boring? What mood are you trying to establish? It doesn't have to be anything fancy. Just let your personality show through a little, and make your students feel at home.

173. Normalize tough moments by talking about them ahead of time.

Students can be emotionally fragile sometimes. A difficult test, a speech, and other high-pressure situations can really make them freak out. Try to normalize these situations by talking about strategies to deal with them. Make them be less of a surprise for students. Admit that it may get tough. When they know something difficult is coming ahead of time, it can be a lot easier to deal with.

174. Don't take up too much class time dealing with a behavior issue.

There are only so many minutes that you get with your students in a given year. You should value them preciously. Yes, classroom management is important, but try to never let it dominate the time you have in a given period. Create an organized and efficient system of discipline, and make it your goal to deal with student misbehavior as quickly as possible.

175. Be able to change gears in your teaching personality.

The best teachers have a variety of different personas that they can go to. This does not mean that they are not being authentic, it simply means that they may need to use different parts of their personality to fit different situations. For instance, if you are a teacher and a coach, you might have very different personas to fit each job. You might even be different from class to class depending on students' age, level, or behavior. So don't feel bad if you find yourself having multiple personalities during your school day. Being able to do so is a plus. Just be sure you can keep all of your personalities straight!

Story Time: When I was in high school, I was a teacher's assistant for one period of the day. My job was to sit in the back of a class and grade papers for the teacher. During my time doing this job, I had an eye-opening experience. I noticed that my teacher, who was super cool and laid back during my senior level honors class, was strict and extremely serious for this class (which was a much younger group of students). He had an almost completely different personality. I realized that teachers sometimes have to act differently depending on the level and ages of the students in the class they are teaching. So, have your different personality styles ready to go. You may even have to change them in the middle of the same school year for some classes.

176. Teach the mental side of test taking as well as content.

There is a lot riding on tests in the current world of education—both for students and teachers. Teaching the mental side of taking tests and general test-taking strategies is always a good addition to your content instruction. Things like handling test anxiety, managing time, and other test-taking strategies could be very useful skills for students in the heavy-testing environment they find themselves in these days.

Story Time: I have always been a pretty good test taker. I think this is one of the main reasons I was able to get into a decent college. In these times of high stakes test taking, it is always good to give your students a few tips about the mental side of it. So what was my secret? When I was taking tests, I always tried to only be concerned about the things I knew. Instead of getting stressed out and fretting about the things I didn't know on a test, I just tried to make sure I got the parts right that I did know. When you can be completely focused on what you know, it is much easier to do your best on tests.

177. Be relentless about getting students placed appropriately.

It does not matter how good your teaching skills are if your students are not in the appropriate class level for their abilities. This is especially true for incremental classes like math and foreign language, but it is important for every subject. If students aren't in the right class level, they will likely become behavior problems (whether the class is too hard or too easy), and they will also potentially hold back the class if they are slower than the rest of the students.

178. Don't "give" grades.

Some educators have become such grade worshipers these days that the grades are often an end to themselves. As a result, it can be tempting for teachers to "cook the books" and give students grades they may *need*. Don't be one of those teachers. Use grades for what they were originally intended for—as a measurement of learning and performance. When you give a student a grade because of the benefit that grade will have for the student instead of to reflect what the student actually did, you are cheating the system, the student, and yourself.

179. Don't offer test corrections.

If you find yourself feeling like you have to do something to save your students' grades on tests, you are probably not making your tests fair enough. Instead of having the grade safety-net of test corrections for students, how about making sure your tests are more valid? Once you have accomplished that, then it is the responsibility of the students to do what is necessary to perform on your tests or deal with the consequences of a poor grade.

If you absolutely *must* do test corrections, make them a low percentage of the overall grade. The experience of having to deal with pressure is good practice for students. Don't bail them out from having to deal with test pressure with the safety net of being able to recover a large part of a bad grade.

180. Make sure your grading system is fair.

Setting up a fair grading system can be a major challenge, especially for nonmath people. If you don't have much comfort with numbers and statistics, you might want to get someone to help you figure out a good grading system. Make sure that you carefully plan how you want things like tests, homework, projects, and so on to be weighted. Also, if your school uses a computer program to set up grades, you definitely need to be sure you have it set up exactly how you want. It is important to have a grading system that is fair and that represents students' grades the way you intend.

181. Be careful how you curve grades.

Ah, the good old test-grade curve. It has been a favorite of teachers forever. The thinking behind curving grades is clear:

if a test was too hard, maybe the scores should be adjusted to make the results more representative of students' knowledge. Curving grades is not necessarily automatically a bad practice, just be sure that you figure out a fair and reasonable way to do it. You don't want to skew grades among students in your class and make the spread unfair because you made a screwy curve.

182. Don't have grade cutoffs or minimums.

Some teachers (and even schools) have minimum grade cutoffs built into their grading setup. For instance, nothing lower than fifty would be given as a failing grade. WARNING! Math ahead:

If a student answers all of the questions correctly on one test and then none of the answers correctly on the next test with the same number of questions, then the student knows half of the material. If there was a minimum grade rule in place (i.e., no zeros allowed), the average would be inflated above fifty.

The problem with this setup is that it does not reflect true student performance and knowledge. If you start messing with scores just to make things friendlier for students, their grades will be artificially inflated. Stop cooking the books just to save students' grades and feelings. The grade should represent the student's actual performance, not the grade that would make the student feel the best about him- or herself.

183. Don't let students be satisfied with just passing.

Some students have a goal of just trying to do enough to pass. Instead of trying to do their best, they merely want to meet the minimum requirement to get by. Don't let these kinds of comments go unaddressed. One of your duties as a teacher is to try to inspire students to always make their best effort. Don't let them be satisfied with making the lowest effort possible to barely pass.

184. Don't pass students who haven't earned it.

A high school diploma has long been a measuring stick for employers. In the past, not having a high school diploma would make you ineligible for certain jobs. Makes sense to me. Employers wanted to see that you at least had some ability, knowledge, work ethic, and so on.

Unfortunately, this system has become a little warped. There is now some "cooking the books" going on so to speak. Since schools know that a degree will help students in the "real world," there is now a temptation to give them a diploma even if they don't earn it. The reason for this gift-giving approach is that these students wouldn't make it without being able to get these jobs. So instead of having higher expectations or holding students to a higher standard, many schools are now resigned to just give out diplomas like candy. These days, just about all you have to do to get a high school diploma is show up enough and try.

185. Give students a chance to earn bonus points.

Bonus points can have a number of benefits. For one, they can give your higher-achieving students something to do if they finish their classwork before other students. They can give students opportunities to go above and beyond the normal course content if they are intellectually curious. Bonus points can also help your lower-achieving students by giving them a chance to improve their grade. Bonus opportunities can be a very good thing. Just be careful about putting too much weight on them. You don't want a bonus to be a replacement for the normal work that is required for the class.

Chapter Five

Wisdom

Anyone who spends twenty plus years in the classroom is bound to learn a few things along the way. I have learned from other teachers, from my own experiments, and from mistakes. Hopefully some of my insights in this section will be helpful.

186. Know when it's time to change careers.

It is never good to hate your job. No matter how good the cause of teaching is, it can be very tough. A career in education is definitely not for everyone, and even if it is right for you for a little while, it may not be good for you for the long term. If you are starting to dread having to go in every day, regardless of how long you have been teaching, it might be a good idea to think of doing something else.

187. Don't complain about salary.

Every now and then you may hear teachers complain about the money they make. This is on my list of pet peeves in the teaching profession. There are two good answers for complaints like this: (1) Unless you are teaching in a private school, you aren't producing any money. Any pay you do get is a gift from the government. (2) Nobody forced you to become a teacher. You knew what you were getting into. If you are dying to make more money, find something else to do. Just stop complaining about teacher salaries like you are some kind of victim.

188. Be careful what you post online.

A common piece of advice is to only post online what you would comfortable posting on a big billboard in town. This is not a bad way to think about it. Despite what you might think, social media sites are not just limited to your friends. Anything that you publish online is public record and can be used against you. Be very careful about posting anything that even has a hint of being inappropriate.

189. Don't get set in your ways.

If you haven't noticed, there are *major* changes taking place in education—from online classes to Internet access to changes in discipline and much more. Don't be the type of teacher who is so set in your ways that you want to keep doing everything like you did in 1991. Sometimes you may not like the new way of doing things. Yes, sometimes the old ways are better. But at least be open to the idea that something new may actually be an improvement. At some point, you may have no choice but to conform to it if you want to stay in the profession.

190. Don't embarrass yourself in public.

This one seems like it should be common sense, but be careful what you are doing in public. When you become a teacher, you have eyes on you 24/7 (and you can be recorded these day too). It is almost like you have a celebrity status. You cannot afford to think of teaching as a nine-to-five job that you just show up to and leave behind at the end of the day. Be careful not to do anything *too* crazy (especially if you like to enjoy a little alcohol every now and then).

Story Time: A teacher friend once told me a story that made me rethink the way I acted in public. He was a high school teacher in South Carolina, and he was on a summer vacation in Europe. While eating in a restaurant, he heard someone say "Mr. _____!" It turned out that one of his students was eating at the same restaurant! So, even if you are thousands of miles away from home, there is still a chance you will be seen by someone connected to your school. Something to think about the next time you are out in public deciding if you want to act a little crazy or do something you want to keep secret.

191. Don't assume that everything old is bad and everything new is good.

There seems to be a trend in education lately to do out with the old and in with the new. Any traditional way of doing things is under attack, while new ideas and methods are championed as the best thing since sliced bread. Maybe it is time to slow down a little and make sure that common sense is still being used. Progress is great, but that doesn't mean that just because an idea is new that it's good. Be careful about jumping on the bandwagon of change just for the sake of change.

192. Filter every decision you make by asking yourself if it is best for students.

Sometimes the stresses of teaching can put you in survival mode and change your focus from your students to yourself. You may feel like working as little as possible and leaving as quickly as you can. Don't let this happen to you. Any decision you make should not be about what makes things easier for you or what makes your reputation better. It should be about what is best for your students. Hopefully the two can go hand in hand. If they don't, though, always choose what benefits students the most.

193. Don't take the day off on your birthday.

Don't be frivolous about taking days off unless you really need to. You are paid to do the best job you can. There are plenty of off days during the school year as it is.

194. Try to avoid meeting with parents alone (especially angry ones).

If you teach long enough, you will have to deal with an irate parent or two. Instead of fearing these kinds of situations, be ready for them. Cover yourself. If you know a parent meeting is coming, try to have a coworker present in case someone needs to corroborate what was said or not said. Know ahead of time that you want to keep your cool if a parent gets upset with you. The main thing to avoid with parents is getting into a heated, back-and-forth kind of argument or dispute. Nobody ever wins in those situations.

195. Never be alone with a student in your room with the door closed.

It is a shame that you have to worry about these things, but that is the world in which we live. Protecting yourself against a possible accusation is always a good idea, even if you have to go a little overboard. One way to do this is to try to never be alone with an individual student in your classroom. If there is no way to avoid it, but *sure* that you at least leave the door open. Don't give the student any opening to falsely accuse you of anything inappropriate. It doesn't matter how honorable you might be, all it takes is one accusation by a student to significantly damage your reputation.

196. Don't be afraid to grade in red ink.

Ugh. There are actually teachers making the case to do away with grading in red because it is just too harsh for students. Good grief. Trying to protect students from everything that is even potentially uncomfortable is not doing them any favors.

197. Choose your words carefully.

One of the most surprising things about students is that they often have very good memories. And I'm not talking about their ability to memorize content. No, some students will remember *anything* you say, even if you thought it was insignificant. Harsh words, compliments, funny comments, and everything else is fair game to stick into the long-term memory of your students. So measure your words like they are being recorded. Some of them will stay with your students for a very long time.

198. Save all e-mails from parents.

You never know when you will need to bring up proof of a conversation. Protect yourself and save it all. There are a lot of crazy parents out there.

199. E-mail parents instead of calling them.

Having conversations through e-mail instead of a phone call leaves a record. This may sound a little paranoid, but you never know when you might need proof of something later. Can you tell how important I think it is to cover yourself against possible complaints?

200. Single teachers: date during the summer.

Teaching can be *very* hard on your social life. You don't meet many new people like you might in other jobs. You can easily get worn out both mentally and physically and just want to veg out on the weekends. And that does not even take into account the mood that teaching can get you into. So if you are a single person and you would rather not stay single, take advantage of those free summer months. You may not have many opportunities during the school year.

201. Don't add students on Facebook until they graduate.

There is just something a little strange about having connections with current students on social media. Play it safe and don't let them add you until after they have graduated. It is always in your best interests to avoid any chance of doing anything that looks inappropriate.

202. Chat with random teachers on social media.

You might be surprised at how many educators are on social media. Some of them are *really* into it. You don't necessarily have to be on every social media site out there, but there does seem to be a large number of educators on Twitter. You may also want to take a look at Facebook, although Twitter does seem to be more conducive to talking to strangers. You can search people you know or well-known educators, and you can also get into chats where educators discuss every topic imaginable. There is a lot of wisdom out there, and many educators are willing to share it.

203. Stay in the same state.

If you are planning on teaching for a long time, it is a good idea to try to teach in the same state. Some retirement systems won't let you transfer money and/or time credit from state to state. Try to stay with the same one if you can, even if you change schools.

204. Conserve your energy.

Sit down when you can. Be efficient with your trips to the office to make copies. No matter how old you are, it is always a good idea to be aware of chances to conserve energy during the day. Nobody likes getting home from a day of teaching and being completely spent, especially when it could have been prevented.

Chapter Six

Relationships with Students

Most teachers are in the profession because they love students. They want to help students succeed. They might be good at their content area and have good intentions but may not always be great at making connections with their students and forming great relationships. Forming great relationships with your students will not only make things more pleasant for everyone involved, but it will also have the side benefit of bringing out the best in your students (and yourself).

205. Don't show other teachers your class roster at the start of the year to try to find out who the "bad" kids are.

Teachers can sometimes be paranoid. The fear that your class will be full of misbehaving students can be a great cause of stress. Why not try to dig up as much dirt as you can on your future students so you can get mentally prepared, right? While this strategy may be logical, it may not be the best idea for getting off to a good start with your students. Instead of judging your students before you even meet them, give students a clean slate and an open mind instead (and tell them this on the first day). Make a dependable classroom management plan and you won't have to worry about future misbehaving students.

206. Do what you say you are going to do.

There are few things that will make you lose your credibility with students faster than not doing something you said you were going to do. Breaking a promise to students can end whatever relationship you may have formed with them—no matter how big or small the promise was. If for some reason something does come up and you have no choice but to break your word, be sure that you are extremely apologetic to your students and be willing to do whatever you can to make up for it. Whatever you do, be sure that you make it a priority to keep your word with students. It can make or break you. It is that big of a deal.

207. Avoid oversharing too much personal information with your students.

Don't treat your class like they are your personal therapy group. Teachers and students can form close relationships, without a doubt. Just don't get so comfortable with your class that you start sharing your personal issues like they were your close friends. Yes, you should love your students like they are your family. You are still an authority, though. Don't weird them out by talking about inappropriate things that are happening in your life. Do your best to keep your relationships with students professional.

208. Go to extracurricular events.

Most students *love* it when their teachers show up at a ball game, play, or other extracurricular event. Little things like this show you care, and that is a major deal to students. Bonus points if you praise them and/or talk about it in class the next day.

209. Get to know students better.

You don't have to be nosy about it, but try to get to know your students as more than just test-taking robots. Let down your guard a little and let them get to know you too.

210. Pay attention to what you wear to work.

There are a wide variety of opinions these days about the importance of what we wear to work. Some think that dressing professionally has a major impact on performance, and some think it makes no difference at all. Dressing "casual" may not be a big deal if you work at Google, but when you are an authority figure, what you wear has a direct impact on your image with students. Not only that, but the way you dress can also affect your mind-set. How you select your wardrobe may not be the most important part of being a successful teacher, but why not give yourself every advantage that you can get?

211. Don't play favorites.

Kids can be sensitive. Believe it or not, even the most misbehaving students often care a lot about what their teachers think of them. Keeping this in mind, you should try very hard not to play favorites or even give the appearance that you might be.

You will have a lot more peace and harmony in your class if students don't think you like other students better.

212. Don't hold grudges against students.

If a student misbehaves or has a bad behavior day, don't keep punishing them over and over again by holding a grudge. Students will appreciate knowing that a bad day won't be held over them forever, so go out of your way to tell them that this is the case. This does not mean that you have to completely forget what they did or even that you aren't going to hold them accountable for their actions. Just give students a chance to start with a clean slate at the beginning of each day.

213. Don't be afraid to criticize students.

Students need to learn how to deal with failure and criticism. Don't be one of these teachers who is afraid to say anything negative out of fear that their students won't be able to handle it. One of the reasons that some students can't handle difficulty is because so many adults in their life have tried to protect them so much from anything difficult or uncomfortable. To be clear, this is not to suggest that you be mean to students just for the sake of doing so. Just don't shy away from constructive criticism if you think the student will benefit from it.

214. Don't feel like you have to win every argument/dispute.

Sometimes it's better to try to be the bigger man (or woman) when conflict arises. This might mean that you have to occasionally swallow your pride, brush off an insult, or in some way let something go. In the grand scheme of things, you are often better off not digging in and trying to win every argument at all costs.

215. Make good eye contact.

Making good eye contact is social skills 101. It may not seem like a big deal, but students notice these kinds of things. Make good eye contact with students when you are addressing the entire class by moving around from student to student and holding his or her gaze for a second. You may be surprised how much of a difference this kind of thing can make to students.

Story Time: One of my traditions when I was teaching was to have students fill out information cards on the first day of class. This would help me get to know the students better and help me learn their names. I would ask them things like, "What is your favorite TV show?" and "Where else have you lived?" One question I always asked was "Have you heard anything about me or this class?"

As you might guess, I would often get some random answers to this question. One year a student wrote, "I heard you don't make enough eye contact with students." Wow! So not only did students care enough about the amount of eye contact the teacher made with them, but they cared enough to tell their friends about it! You never know what might be important to students. I learned the hard way that eye contact is on the list.

216. Prepare students for their future.

Don't let yourself get so caught up in your daily lessons that you forget about the big picture. Be sure you consider the next class, next grade, college, career, or whatever is coming for your students. Too many teachers teach their class like they think it is the only class the students will ever take.

217. Grade and return papers quickly.

Sometimes what seem like little things can make a big difference. Students appreciate it when you grade and return papers quickly. Even more so, they think badly of you when you don't grade quickly. Don't be lazy. Make it a priority to communicate with students about their performance as soon as possible.

218. Don't compare students to siblings (out loud or to yourself).

If you teach long enough, you will likely have siblings of former students in your class at some point. Be careful not to assume that brothers and sisters will behave (or think or work) in a similar way. They can be very different! Siblings are probably tired of being compared to their brothers or sisters, especially if one was a high achiever. So when you get that roster at the beginning of the year and you see a familiar last name, don't assume that people from the same family will act similarly or have similar intelligence. They may very well surprise you.

219. Don't talk about other classes to your students.

Even though they may try to act cool, students can be sensitive! Many of them don't want to think that you like another student (or class) better than you like them. So be considerate and try to avoid talking to students about other classes. Let your students feel like they are your whole world.

220. Stand up for students with special needs.

Kids can be mean about teasing. So mean that it will break your heart sometimes. One of the favorite targets of people who like to make fun of others is those who are different. Be on the lookout for this kind of behavior. You should be putting a stop to any kind of bullying, of course, but there is just something extra terrible about making fun of a special needs–type student.

It can be easy to get wrapped up in the duties of your school day and not notice kids who are picking on other kids without being dramatically obvious about it. This is why you should make an effort to seek it out and be ready to shut down any hint of this awful behavior as soon as you notice it. Terrible.

221. Say hello and goodbye to your students.

Little things make a difference. Will saying hello and goodbye to students instantly make you beloved and solve all of your student behavior problems? Probably not. But every little bit of positive energy you can bring helps.

222. Have fun with your students.

Some teachers feel like they have to be serious every second of every day. It doesn't have to be this way. It's okay to let down your hair a little every now and then and joke and cut up with your students (or maybe even more than every now and then). Some teachers still have the notion that you better not smile in class or you won't be effective. Or don't smile until Christmas, as the old saying goes. Hogwash. You don't have to act like a crazy goofball, but letting out a little of your personality and having fun won't automatically kill your classroom management. Just make sure you make it clear to your students that there are times when being serious is necessary.

223. Lightly tease your (older) students after you get to know them.

Some say that imitation is the best form of flattery. You could also make the case that teasing is a great compliment as well. How could that be? For whatever reason, people often tease those they like most. You have to be really careful about how you go about your teasing, of course, because you don't want it to get offensive. It is okay to needle your students a little once you get to know them, though. It actually shows that you like them while at the same time showing that you aren't going to be one of these teachers who sugarcoats all the time. Just use your common sense with this one. You may not want to do this if you teach first graders, who wouldn't understand what you were doing. Some older students will appreciate it, though.

224. Show students respect.

There are some teachers who could solve most of their discipline problems if they just respected students more. Respect is a key part of successful discipline, if not the most important part. Let's put an end to the popular thinking that teachers have to be mean or angry to be successful with classroom management. Students wanted to be treated fairly and reasonably, not like second-class citizens.

225. Don't treat high schoolers like children.

One of the biggest mistakes that teachers make is treating their students like they are about a year or two younger than they really are. This is especially true in high school. Don't you realize that a high school student is only a year or two away from being in college, going to work, or being in the military? Instead of babying them and treating them like children, do them a favor and start to think of them like young adults. They will be better off for it.

226. Compliment students publicly.

It is amazing how powerful a teacher's words are to students. Things that you may not think are a big deal can be a big deal to them. Complimenting students in class or in other public ways can really make them feel good. Just be sure you don't get weird about it and compliment inappropriate things like looks, clothes, and so forth.

227. Be real with your students.

Most students seem to appreciate it when you are real with them. Be willing to correct students and occasionally tell them the hard truth and your compliments will carry more weight.

228. Tell students stories about your life.

Students like to know that their teachers are real people. Telling a story every now and then about your life or something you like to do can help build your relationship with them. Just don't get carried away and take *too* much time talking about yourself in class.

229. Think of and treat students like family.

The teachers who enjoy their job the most and who have the most success are often the ones who love their students and show it. Enough said.

230. Avoid inappropriate humor with students.

Oh, the temptation to try hard to be cool and liked by students. It can cause so many problems for teachers. It is completely fine to kid and joke with your students every now and then, but try to be careful what you joke about. The desire to be a good role model should be stronger than the desire to be liked. Not to mention that with the way everything is being recorded these days, it is probably a good idea not to say something you don't want replayed in front of a parent or administrator.

231. Keep your political beliefs to yourself.

Students may be able to figure out your political leanings if they pay attention to what you talk about. Some things you just can't hide, so be very careful about directly stating what you believe when it comes to politics. Let students make up their own minds in this area.

232. Don't have bad breath.

Be considerate of your students. You may be spending a lot of time in close proximity to them during a typical school day. Slight dehydration is a big cause of bad breath, so drink plenty of water (especially after you have had coffee). A mint every now and then wouldn't hurt either. You're welcome, students.

233. Don't use your phone in the middle of class.

Unless you allow students to use their phones during class, it is probably not a good idea to use yours either unless it is an emergency or for something school related. You are obviously in charge as the teacher, and you can do mostly whatever you want, but students are in love with their phones these days. Don't rub it in that you can use yours and they can't use theirs.

234. Don't flaunt your power.

Teachers should have a different set of rules to follow than students. The roles are different. It is probably not a good idea to flaunt that power, though. Nobody likes leaders who rub their power in your face. It is probably not a good idea to be drinking soda, talking on your phone, and so on in front of the students if those are things that you can get away with doing but they can't.

235. Don't feel pressure to talk content every second of every day.

The content that you are required to teach is important, there is no doubt about it. It is okay to take a short break from your content every now and then, though. Don't feel guilty if you go off track occasionally and have a little fun or get to know your students a little better. There is plenty of time for content.

236. Learn your students' names quickly.

You may not realize it, but students care how much their teachers care! The saying goes that the best thing a person can hear is their own name. Remember that.

237. Love students without needing to be loved back.

You will never be able to serve your students as well as you could if you depend on them loving you. They should not have to earn your attention, care, and service. What if a student just doesn't like you? Does he or she deserve less of your effort? Certainly not. So love them unconditionally. If they love you, great. If not, love them anyway.

238. Understand that some students will hate you just because you are a teacher.

Some students (and parents) have a terrible history with teachers. They may have been yelled at, harassed, or even worse by past teachers. So don't take it personally when students have a negative opinion of you before they even get to know you. Take it as a challenge to try to change their opinions about teachers after seeing how well you treat them.

239. Make it a goal that students feel safe and comfortable in your class.

It seems that teachers sometimes don't realize how important it is for students to feel safe in their classroom. It should be a priority to make sure that no students have any fear of another student bothering them or of the teacher bothering them. Students can't be their best if they are afraid or stressed out about what might be said or done to them in class.

240. Make sure you are fair with students you don't like.

If you teach for long enough, you will come across students that you don't like. Gasp! It is true. Some people just don't get along, and some of your students may act like flat-out jerks to you. If there is a student you don't get along with, be sure that you still do your best to be as fair as possible. No matter how badly he or she may act toward you, it is still your job to teach that student as best as you can.

241. Realize that some students may have teacher-hating parents.

Sometimes a student's hate for teachers in general may come from his or her parents. This can be a difficult situation to recover from. There is no point in worrying about it. All you can do is treat all of your students well and hope they appreciate you. If they don't, they don't.

242. Talk about school sports and other extracurricular activities in class.

Many students *love* it when they know a teacher comes to their games, performances, and so on. Do your best to go to events, and even better, make sure you complement your students in front of the class for their performance. Make a comment even if you couldn't make it but heard about something great they did. You will score big.

243. Take the students' side whenever you can.

Students will sometimes get in trouble and you will be asked to give a character reference for them to an administrator. This is not to say that you have to turn a blind eye to the truth, but always try to give your students the benefit of the doubt when they find themselves in trouble. Have their back and they will have yours too. You may be the only one who does.

244. Teach students life lessons.

Having students score well on standardized tests is great, but you can also impact their lives by teaching life lessons. Things like work ethic, manners, social skills, and so on are all skills that students can also learn at school. The complete teacher teaches these immeasurable skills with the overall success of their students in mind.

245. Be available after and/or before school often.

It is good when teachers can stay after school to help students as much as possible. Just don't feel obligated. There is no reason to feel guilty if there are days you can't stay or if you don't stay because you need a break.

246. Praise students to their parents when you can.

Complimenting students to their parents can mean a lot to both the parent and student—especially if they are used to always getting bad news. So look for chances to say something nice when you can. Just make sure you mean it. Don't feel like you have to be fake.

247. Don't post honor rolls.

Teachers, schools, and newspapers who publicize honor rolls and grades have good intentions—to celebrate students' achievement. Sounds like a great idea, right? Not so fast. Every student may not want their grades published. For one, some kids don't think it is cool to be smart, and they don't want it known that they are. Some people just don't like having their business made public, no matter how good it is.

248. Avoid sarcasm (unless you are being obviously funny).

Sarcasm is often used for one of two purposes: either to be funny or to insult someone. Teachers who use sarcasm a lot should be very careful that their meaning for it is clearly communicated. Many times lower-level students or younger students may not understand it, which means they are just going to take you literally. That may not be good depending on how you are using your sarcasm. Sometimes it is best just to avoid it.

249. Make sure you don't favor girls or boys.

Let's face it, unless you are just mean to all of your students all the time, some of them are going to think you play favorites. This is unavoidable. All you can do is to try to be intentional about treating all students fairly and try not to send the message that you like some better than others. If you get the sense that a student feels like you are playing favorites, you may want to explain to the class or individual that you love all of your students equally and do your best not to give any special treatment.

250. Explain to students the realities of building a reputation with teachers.

People in the business world often talk about building a "brand" for themselves. Students and teachers do the same thing in a school. Your brand is your reputation. If you build a brand of being well mannered and cooperative with teachers, you will have a better chance of getting along with them. The same is true for teachers. If you build a reputation for being mean to students, that can hurt students' opinions of you before they even know you.

251. Don't get lecture-y when giving consequences.

Teenagers are known for tuning out adults who lecture them. It is always best to let your consequences speak for themselves. You don't need to subject your students to both your consequence *and* a sermon about it.

252. Be quick to forgive.

Let's not overuse the "they are only kids" excuse for bad behavior, but we all make mistakes. Unless a student does something *really* bad to you, it is usually a good idea to forgive them as quickly as possible. If the student earns a consequence for the bad behavior, give it to them and move on. Forgive and forget as much as possible.

253. Give students a chance to correct their issues before you call home.

There are times as a teacher when you may feel powerless to make a difference or improve a student's misbehavior. In these cases, you may be tempted to call the parents and see if they can help. While this may be an appropriate and effective response at times, it is usually better to give students a chance to change their bad behavior before you decide to call home. Hold out for as long as you can before involving the parents. Not only will this teach students to be responsible for their own actions, but it can also keep you from being the bad guy who told on them. Feel free to call parents if you feel like there is no other choice, but do not use the parent phone call as your automatic answer to every discipline problem you face.

254. Talk about your desire to help students win in life, not just pass the class.

Motivation is a big part of teaching. If you can convince your students that you want to help them succeed in life and not just in your class or on the year-end test, you will probably make a much greater impact.

255. Always be ready to tell students why you are teaching what you are teaching.

Sometimes the content in a class is directly useful to students, sometimes it's not. Sometimes the skills they learn are important, and sometimes just the general practice of using their brains is what matters. Whatever the case may be in your class, always be ready to give an explanation for why you are teaching something. "Learning how to learn" is always a good answer when you don't have a great explanation to give for teaching a particular topic.

256. Try to let students save face during a dispute in front of other students.

Students are often very concerned about their reputation. Your relationships with students will be improved tremendously if you just fix this one thing: try not to embarrass students in front of their peers. Choose your words carefully when you have a dispute with a student during class, and take them into the hall to talk privately if needed. Just do whatever it takes to avoid publicly shaming them. They may not show it immediately, but they will appreciate that you did that for them.

257. Don't hold grudges.

This tip is very important, especially if you teach students who tend to misbehave a lot. They want to know that they can have a chance to make up with you if they mess up. If you want to form any kind of relationship whatsoever with this type of student, you must have a short memory. If students break a rule, give them a consequence and let them have a clean slate. But don't keep bringing it up, even in your own mind. Let them know that once they pay their penalty, it is forgiven and forgotten. Try to avoid holding grudges against students unless they do something *really, really* bad to you. Most student misbehavior doesn't fall into that category.

258. Look for the good in every student.

Contrary to the message that is often sent in the media, most people are probably mostly good. As a teacher, you can help your peace of mind if you focus on this idea. And if you have students who might be making you doubt their goodness, dig a little deeper. Everyone has some good in them. Some students just need a teacher who is willing to look for it and not be quick to assume that they are bad.

Chapter Seven

Relationships with Other Teachers

Schools that have teachers who get along are more positive places. It's as simple as that. When teachers don't get along, the negative energy spreads through the school. It may take an intentional effort, but forming better relationships with coworkers just has a way of making the job better.

259. Don't get overly competitive with other teachers.

Teachers can have some really hateful fights over everything from test scores and grades to homecoming competitions. Don't let yourself be one of those teachers. Sometimes it is a good idea to remind yourself that you are there for the kids, not to show off or win your own personal battles. Come on, people.

260. Go out of your way to get along with coworkers.

Teaching is hard enough without having to deal with conflict with your fellow teachers. Do whatever it takes to get along with them. If that means that you may have to swallow your pride over something, do it. If that means underreacting to something that probably deserves an angry response, do it.

If conflict just cannot be avoided, try to be as calm and respectful as possible. Get in a room with the teacher you have problems with and air it out. If you are afraid that things might get heated, try to find another coworker to sit in on the conversation. Whatever you do, though, don't let the tension broil under the surface without dealing with it. That is a good way to make your life at school miserable.

261. Don't be too cliquish.

Everyone knows people who they get along better with than others. And it is only natural that people who teach similar subjects are more likely to connect with each other. Don't limit yourself to only the like-minded, though. Get to know people who might be a little different than you. Chat with teachers who are in different grades, subject areas, or levels. There is nothing wrong with having your best friends be the people who are most similar to you. But be careful not to avoid people just because they don't fit with one of your cliques.

262. Look out for coworkers who need help.

I've said it before and I'll say it again—teaching is hard. You are better off if you don't have to go through it alone. There is something nice about having a school culture where teachers look out for each other. Cover for your fellow teacher when he or she is sick. Offer an idea about something that worked for you. Just generally be as helpful as possible. It makes for a much happier, more productive work environment.

263. Don't insult other teachers during class.

Teachers can be so competitive! Don't let yourself fall into the slimy situation of insulting other teachers to your students. Ugh. You may feel superior when you do that, and you may just love to gossip, but nothing but harm can come from this practice. Don't let yourself get into the "I am great and they're not" type of attitude with your students. And while we are on this topic, don't let students talk negatively about other teachers either (no matter how true the discussions might be). Do what you can to be unified with your fellow teachers.

264. Don't gossip.

Gossiping about negative drama can suck the positive energy right out of your school. Don't let yourself participate in it. You know you wouldn't want people to say negative things about you, so don't do say it about them either. If you aren't sure if something is too negative or even if it seems like it might be neutral, avoid the topic. This includes talking about other teachers, students, staff, and anyone else.

265. Don't brag excessively about your accomplishments.

Nobody cares.

266. Don't brag excessively about your own children.

Nobody wants to hear it.

267. Help other teachers when they ask for it.

If you have taught for any length of time, it should not be difficult to have some empathy for your fellow teachers. Bend over backward to help them if you have to. Not only will you be doing a good deed, but you never know when you might need a favor yourself. Build a good reputation for helping your coworkers and you are more likely to receive help when you need it.

268. Show your appreciation when your coworkers do something nice for you.

Do you ever ask another teacher to cover your class when you have to leave early for a dental appointment or to coach or for some other reason? If he or she covers for you, show appreciation! Even a small piece of candy can work wonders. Spread that positive energy!

269. Do random acts of kindness for your coworkers.

Building positive energy at school is so important. It can make a huge different for both students and teachers. Do what you can to make this happen—bring in food for your coworkers at lunchtime, buy raffle tickets for their students' fund-raisers, whatever it takes. Get creative if you have to. The benefits of having positive relationships at school far outweigh whatever costs or inconveniences they may cause.

270. Don't be jealous of other teachers.

There are a lot of great teachers out there. Some take twenty years to become great, and some can't help but be great early. Don't let successful teachers make you feel bad about where you are in your career. Focus on being the best that you can be, and don't worry about what others might be doing. You will have a lot more energy and peace that way.

271. Don't make so much noise in your class that it bothers nearby classes.

Be considerate of teachers and classes around you. Many classrooms are separated by walls that don't offer much sound protection. Yes, your classroom is your domain, and you want to be able to do whatever you want, but if you are disrupting other classes, then you probably need to get things a little more under control. If you know that you are going to have a day that might be a little noisier than usual, at least have the courtesy to warn teachers near you.

272. Ask teachers for advice.

Teachers love to feel important. And a lot of them have opinions on just about anything. Ask for their advice whenever you need some help and they will usually be more than willing to assist you. You may feel like you are being annoying, but most of the time you will be stroking their ego.

273. Have a short memory about arguments and disputes.

This is a good tip for dealing with students too, but it is also true for your relationships with coworkers. Everyone has disagreements and even arguments at times. Unless the argument was over something *really* terrible and personal, have your argument and move on. Don't let things that are not really that important ruin good relationships.

274. Carpool.

Sharing the drive to school has a lot of benefits. It saves money. It grows relationships. It can help you keep things in perspective. Yes, it may be a little more inconvenient than driving yourself, but it may be worth the trouble. Just be considerate and agree not to talk about work the *whole time* on the drive to and from school.

275. Sit with different people at lunch.

Get to know your coworkers. Sit with different people at lunch if you have the option, or eat at different times. Don't be satisfied with your same old routine and your same old relationships.

276. Don't eat alone.

They say that eating with people is better for your digestion and health. That is good enough reason for me not to eat alone! Eating with other people will also grow relationships. There is something almost magical about the bonding that takes place when eating with someone.

277. Be careful what you send over the school e-mail or look at on your school computer.

This one shouldn't even have to be stated, but unfortunately teachers sometimes make mistakes in this area. Just realize that everything you e-mail or look at on your school computer or through your school Wi-Fi is being watched. Don't do anything stupid.

278. Say hello to coworkers when you pass in the hallway.

Little things matter, especially when it comes to positivity. Take advantage of every chance for positive energy you can find. Say hello, good morning, and so on when you pass your fellow teachers in the hallway (and students you know too). Make small talk when you can. Small attempts at positive energy can add up.

Chapter Eight

Relationships with Administrators

The relationship between teacher and principal is a little different from the typical boss/employee relationship. Teachers are used to being in charge for most of the day, but they also have a boss who is in charge of them. Having the right mindset is the key to making your principals allies instead of enemies.

279. Only ask for help from administration as a last resort.

If you haven't noticed, school administrators are *extremely* busy. The job has insanely long hours, and a lot of them are not fun. So if you are a teacher, don't be a busybody and bother your administrators with issues, complaints, or questions that could be answered elsewhere. There is almost always someone else who can help you anyway.

280. Settle your own disputes with coworkers.

Administrators don't want to have to be your parent or babysitter. If you ever have a dispute with a coworker, do your best to solve it on your own. Let the administrators focus their energy on more important matters.

281. Disagree or complain respectfully.

There will probably be times when you disagree with your administrator. It happens. Sometimes you are better off keeping the disagreement to yourself, and sometimes it is okay to express your complaints to them. There is a good way and a bad way to go about it. Your point will have a much better chance of having an impact if you disagree calmly and respectfully. Also, make sure your disagreement has the purpose of making a positive change, otherwise you are just whining.

282. Don't complain about administrators behind their backs.

If you want to get on your administrators' bad side quickly, say something negative about them behind their back. Not only will it damage the morale in your school, it will also probably get back to the administration. Be smart and make your complaints directly to your administrators, or better yet, don't make them at all. Whatever you do, don't be the teacher who is always complaining about the boss in the faculty lounge.

283. Praise your administrators in class.

A positive school atmosphere takes a total team effort. Little things can make a big difference. Saying negative things about your administrators to your students can undermine their authority and bring down the overall positivity in your school. Like the old saying goes, if you don't have anything nice to say, don't say anything at all.

284. Be welcoming during observations.

Observations are a part of teaching. Instead of making a big deal out of them and stressing out, you are better off embracing them. Don't be afraid to acknowledge whoever is observing you or even include him or her in discussions during class. Make observers feel welcome.

285. Don't tell on other teachers (unless it is about something serious).

Teachers can often act the ages of the students they teach. What an interesting observation. It makes sense that spending so much time around a certain age of student can have an impact on our behavior. It should not be a surprise then that some teachers like to tell on other teachers! Ugh. Let's not lower ourselves to that level. Unless you know of a teacher doing something seriously wrong, leave it alone or find some other way to handle the situation other than telling the boss.

286. Be professional: Don't miss your assigned duties.

Extra duties are often required as part of your job as a teacher. It is better to take these seriously and not miss them if at all possible. Establish a reputation for being dependable and professional.

287. Be professional: Be on time.

Professionalism should be a priority for any teacher. Being on time should be one of the basics. Don't be casual about showing up late to school or being late to class. It may seem like a little thing to you, but the little things can be the difference in establishing a good reputation or a bad one.

288. Be professional: Turn things in on time.

Paperwork is a necessary evil of the teaching profession. Yes, some places require a lot more of it than others. Whatever your requirement for paperwork is, though, make sure you do your best to turn it in on time. This is true for every teacher but especially for new teachers, who should be trying to establish a professional reputation.

289. Be professional: Don't show up as late as possible and leave as early as possible.

Have some pride and respect for yourself and your profession. You are paid to do a job, and you should try to do it as well as possible. Leaving early and coming in late shows that you are only willing to make the minimum effort required to get by.

290. Keep good records.

Grades, attendance, behavior, and so on should all be organized and recorded. You never know when someone might question you about something. The more evidence you have about things that might need checking later, the better.

291. Support new teachers.

Sometimes it's easy to forget how difficult things were when you first started teaching. Teaching can be extremely difficult and stressful, especially for those first three years or so. Do whatever you can to lend a helping hand to teachers who are new to the profession or new to your school. Somebody probably did it for you when you were in the same position. Also, administrators notice when you are a team player.

Chapter Nine

Relationships with Parents

The parent/teacher relationship is an important one. Some parents are very involved in their children's education, and some aren't involved at all. Some parents are very friendly toward teachers, and some are downright hostile. The wise teacher knows how to handle the different types of parents he or she interacts with. The better teachers and parents get along, the better it is for everyone.

292. Don't kiss up to parents.

There should be a spirit of respect and cooperation between teachers and parents. This does not mean that the parents of your students are your bosses, however. Don't feel like you have to kiss up to them. Listen to parents, take their input if you need to, but don't feel like you have to be intimidated by them or worried about what they are going to say or do.

Also, don't be afraid to disagree with a parent about the best way to handle something. You can disagree out of respect and try to come up with the best solution for the problem if you feel that is what is right. If a parent becomes aggressive or belligerent with you in any way, don't hesitate to get an administrator involved in the conversation.

293. Send home a rule/syllabus sheet on first day.

Share your classroom management setup with parents from the beginning so they will know how you will be running your class. The fewer surprises there are when it comes to discipline, the better.

294. Don't think of parents like they are the enemy.

There is story after story of conflict between teachers and parents. This is a shame. It doesn't have to be that way. Instead of working *against* each other, teachers and parents should be working together. Remember, you should both have a common goal: to give the child the best education possible. Keep in mind why you do what you do and it will be easier to get along with parents.

295. Be empathetic with parents.

Try to put yourself in parents' shoes. They are trusting their child to a teacher who they often don't know at all and hoping that the teacher is competent, fair, and reasonable. They may have had bad experiences with teachers from their time in school, or they may have had a bad experience with their children's previous teachers. Sometimes teachers seem to forget that students actually go home and have parents. You aren't the only one who wants what is best for the child. So have some empathy for parents, and treat students like they are your own child. It might change the way you do things.

296. Talk to parents at extracurricular events.

Anything you can do to establish a positive relationship with parents is a good thing. That means being friendly at extracurricular events and talking to them whenever you get the chance. Show that you are a nice person, not just the stereotypical mean old teacher.

297. Keep your composure with angry parents.

If staying calm during heated moments was an Olympic sport, many teachers would be ready to win the gold. Not losing your cool is absolutely essential if you want to have any chance of getting along with parents. Some of them are extremely passionate about their children, and it is hard to blame them for being that way. Don't let yourself get into a battle of back-and-forth yelling, screaming, and anger with parents. Keeping your cool not only will often diffuse a stressful situation, but it will also allow you to keep your self-respect when it's over.

Story Time: During my basketball coaching days, an angry parent once stormed into the locker room during my pregame talk. He wanted to yell at me about his son's lack of playing time. My instinct was to fire back at this crazy person, but I somehow found the strength to keep my composure. I managed to calmly send him away without getting involved in a heated exchange. Another coach who was in the room complemented me on the way I handled the situation. Answering anger with anger is almost always counterproductive. Respond to an angry person with calmness and you will likely come out ahead, and feel good about yourself afterward as well.

298. Return parent calls and e-mails ASAP.

Answering parent calls and e-mails quickly shows them respect. It also tells parents that you think of them as a priority. Little things are big things when it comes to showing a spirit of cooperation and respect.

299. Don't allow impromptu parent meetings.

Don't feel obligated to meet with parents whenever they feel like dropping by. Insist that they respect your time, and make them set up a meeting time later. Not only will this help you save time, but it will also give parents a chance to cool down if they are angry and give you the opportunity to arrange to bring in an observer if needed.

300. Allow parents to sit in on class.

Sometimes parents can't *believe* that their perfect angel of a child would ever misbehave in school. Feel free to invite them to sit in on your class if you think that would help the situation. Granted, this may not be the best way for the parent to see the usual behavior of his or her child, but letting parents come in will at least send a message to students that you are serious about getting them to change their behavior.

Chapter Ten

Advice for Administrators

Have you ever wanted to give feedback to your administrators but were too afraid? Well, I am getting that chance. Here are some insights for the people in charge of teachers that I have learned from both the strengths and weaknesses of principals and assistant principals I have worked for over the years.

301. Don't treat teachers like children.

One of the biggest mistakes that administrators can make is treating their teachers like students. A lot of administrators come from a teaching background, so it is understandable why they might fall into this bad behavior. Their experience usually is mostly with leading kids.

There are a number of reasons why treating teachers like children is a bad idea: (1) Students and employees are two very different things. Teachers are adults, students are not. You can't expect the same methods to work for both groups. (2) Teachers are by nature used to being in charge. They are already a little uncomfortable having someone tell them what to do at all, much less doing it in a way that makes them feel like they are being treated like children. Good administrators realize that the techniques they used as an authority when they were teaching will not be successful when they move to being an authority over teachers.

302. Don't require excessive paperwork from your teachers.

Sorry, teachers, there is some paperwork that is absolutely necessary in the world of education. That is part of the job. This is not what this tip is about. Administrators sometimes seem to have teachers do things that have very little real purpose or benefit. This is a major mistake. Teaching already takes a huge amount of time, effort, and stress. Administrators who don't respect their teachers' time will get very unpopular very quickly.

303. Keep your meetings efficient and as short as possible.

Time efficiency is a skill that not every administrator has, especially when it comes to meetings. Try your best to be as concise as possible. E-mail what you can. Cut out the fluff. Teaching is intense enough on its own without administrators making things worse by wasting their teachers' time.

304. Make professional development useful.

This is simply a case of common sense seemingly not being so common. Administrators should not schedule professional development just so they can say they did something. Make it useful to teachers or don't have it at all.

305. Have an open door for teachers.

From the outside looking in at least, being an administrator is a demanding and time-consuming job. Knowing this, teachers should always appreciate administrators who make themselves available and easily accessible. Make your best effort to be as available as possible for your teachers, even if it is just to let them vent and complain every now and then.

306. Don't guilt trip your teachers into not missing days.

Being a principal is a tremendous challenge, I'm sure. Not only do you have to deal with the issues of a school full of students, but you occasionally have misbehaving teachers as well. You should set boundaries for teachers just like you should for students. If you have teachers who you suspect are missing days frivolously, it is probably wise to address that issue as soon as possible. Teachers should be held to high standards of professionality.

What you should definitely *not* do, however, is make blanket statements to your entire staff trying to make them feel guilty for missing time. Most teachers are professional enough only to miss school when they have to. Making an absence into a "strike" against teachers will only cause stress, resentment, and negative energy. Not to mention the inevitable increase in sickness that will occur when teachers start coming to school sick.

307. Have consequences for teacher misbehavior (and communicate them ahead of time).

Yes, there is a specific tip about not treating teachers like students, but this one is an exception. A rule is not a rule unless there are consequences for not following it. This is true whether you are five years old or an adult. If you want to have nonnegotiable rules as an administrator, there should be consequences for not following them.

The consequence may be something as light as a verbal reminder or as serious as not bringing them back for the next school year. Whatever your consequences are, make sure that you think of them carefully and ahead of time, and make sure your teachers know what the potential consequences are. The worst thing you can do is react and punish in the moment, when you may not be thinking clearly.

308. Praise teachers publicly by name.

Everyone likes to be praised. As the saying goes, the word we like to hear the most is our own name. You aren't going to make or break your relationship with your teachers with this idea, but every little thing can help.

309. Don't blame teachers for student misbehavior.

If there was a ranking of tips from this book in order of importance, this one would probably be near the top of the list. The majority of the responsibility for student misbehavior should belong to the *student*, not the teacher. Yes, teachers can influence students to behave better, and they should be held accountable for doing so. There is no denying that. But there is no teacher who can *completely* control student behavior. If a student is determined to fail and/or misbehave, there is no magic strategy that a teacher can use to stop that student. Blaming the teacher for misbehaving students is an unrealistic and unwise thing to do.

310. Place teachers in their best subject area or grades levels as much as possible.

Here is another one in the common sense not being so common category. To use a sports analogy, wouldn't you want your best players playing in the positions that they are best at? Just like you wouldn't want your kicker playing on the line, you wouldn't want a teacher who was great at teaching math doing social studies. You also wouldn't want to make a teacher who was great with first graders teach fifth graders. Get to know your teachers and get them teaching in their strengths and interests and the success of your school will take off.

311. Ask teachers for input.

The leader who thinks he or she has all the answers will never be as successful as possible. Nobody is able to think of everything. So put aside your pride and encourage your teachers to give you input and suggestions about how things could be better. Sometimes they may have a great idea that you didn't think of.

312. Do random acts of kindness for teachers.

Little things can go a long way. If you want to do something nice for your teachers, you can never go wrong with food. Bring in some donuts or, better yet, a catered lunch and you will be a hero.

313. Dress like a professional.

Set the tone for your school by dressing like the professional you are. This may sound old school, but clothes and appearance can make a difference. This is not to say that your outfit will make or break you, but why not dress for success, as the saying goes. And dressing for success does not necessarily mean that you have to dress in your Sunday best, with a suit and tie or dress. Just wear something that makes you look professional. Dress well, and encourage your teachers to dress well too.

314. Don't visit classrooms excessively.

There are some teachers who will disagree with this tip, but there are also some teachers who *hate* it when administrators visit the classroom. Some like being in their own little world without feeling like they have to filter anything. On the other hand, there are also some teachers who say the opposite—they feel appreciated when their administrators come for a visit. So maybe the best approach would be to get to know your teachers, see what they like, and show appreciation in a way that fits that individual. Just be careful about assuming that all teachers think one way or the other about classroom visits.

315. Take the teacher's side in disputes with parents as much as possible.

Always give your teachers the benefit of the doubt when you can. Unless there is obvious evidence that the teacher was wrong about something, try hard not to assume that he or she is the one at fault. Administrators who are quick to take the parents' side over the teacher's in a dispute are going to do serious damage to their relationship with that teacher. Not to mention the bad reputation that you will get among your co-workers. Considering the much larger amount of time that you will have to spend with teachers compared to parents, you might want to be careful who you choose to support most.

316. Don't make teachers turn in lesson plans.

There are many administrators who think that the dreaded lesson-plan check is a good idea. They might want to think of making a career change. It is that ridiculous. If you are an administrator who requires your teachers to turn in your lesson plans, stop it. Right now. Put down this book immediately and send out a mass e-mail that you are stopping the practice.

Teaching is hard enough without having your principal micromanage you. If you don't trust your teachers enough to make up their own lessons, then you should not have hired them in the first place. Instead of looking over your teachers' shoulders, why not just hire good ones and then let them do their job. There is nothing wrong with checking up on new teachers for their first year or two, but after that it is time to let them be.

317. Try to answer e-mails from your teachers within twenty-four hours.

School administrators are just as busy as teachers, if not more so. You should still make every effort to make your teachers feel like they are heard and respected. Even if you don't agree with a teacher's opinion or refuse his or her request, never let no answer be your "no" answer. Answer teachers' e-mails, their questions, or even just a request to talk to you in person.

318. Don't make mountains out of molehills.

Pick your battles. Some things are just not worth getting worked up about.

319. Don't make teachers speak at meetings unless they want to.

Some administrators might be surprised to know just how much stage fright some teachers have when they are in situations outside of their classroom. Maybe because they aren't in control of the situation, or maybe they are just intimidated by speaking in front of adults after dealing with kids all day. Who knows. But before you ask a teacher to talk at a meeting, realize that some of them may be shaking in their boots at the thought of having to speak at a faculty meeting or in other public situations.

320. Don't be a slave to statistics.

It seems that a lot of educators—from superintendents on down—completely buy into statistics that affect their schools. While it is important to take statistics into consideration when making decisions, it can be dangerous to read *too* much into them. Some data may not always tell the story that it seems to. For instance, graduation rates have been improving in recent years. Does this mean that schools are necessarily teaching students better than they used to? Maybe.

Or maybe schools make it much easier to graduate than they used to (perhaps in effort to make graduation rates look good). The same goes for test scores. Before jumping in and celebrating or condemning teachers or schools over test scores, make sure to dig deeper into what really happened.

Was the test valid? Were there other circumstances that may have causes the scores other than teaching and learning? Learn to at least question statistics before jumping to conclusions and you will have a much more accurate assessment of your school and teachers.

321. Be on the lookout for teachers bullying other teachers.

Sometimes teachers can bully each other just like students do. So be on the lookout. Teachers should not be allowed to get away with it either.

322. Ask about classroom management during interviews.

Bad classroom management equals a bad teacher. Period. There is no way of getting around this. It may seem obvious to ask teachers about classroom management, but sometimes the obvious is not always considered. If you are not in the habit of making classroom management a priority in interviews, you might strongly want to consider doing so. Will some interviewees talk a good game about their classroom management skills but not really know what they are doing? Of course. It is still a good idea to bring up the subject and see what happens. You may get lucky and have some potentially bad hires weed themselves out of the hiring process.

323. Don't make teachers go to extracurricular events.

Teachers should do whatever they can do to support their school. This includes going to extracurricular events. There is no need to force it, though. It doesn't mean as much to students if teachers have no choice but to go to their ball game, plays, concerts, and so on. Hopefully you have hired teachers who buy into having a family-like and supportive atmosphere at your school.

324. Be careful how much special treatment you give to coaches.

Coaching can be extremely time consuming. Some coaches may start their school day at 7 a.m. and not get home from a late-night road game until after midnight. The sports they coach can also bring in a *lot* of money for their schools. It is not hard to see why coaches sometimes get special treatment compared to other teachers. Some special treatment or privileges may be deserved, some not. Just be careful about overdoing it. Other, noncoaching teachers will usually notice the unfairness and may resent you for it.

325. Make your school start no earlier than 8:30 a.m. if you have the power to do so.

Kids need sleep! Making them get up too early can do nothing but harm to their learning and performance. And shouldn't those things be high on the list of priorities for administrators? A later start wouldn't hurt the performance of your teachers either.

326. Make sure students are in the appropriate class level.

The best administrators do whatever they can to make sure that their students are as successful as possible. One often-overlooked way to do this is to make sure that students are in the best class "level"—meaning honors, college prep, remedial, or whatever you call it at your school.

Students who are in the wrong class level already have two strikes against them. Make every effort to ensure that students are where they should be and you will be much closer to helping students be at their best.

327. Don't bend the truth about your school during interviews.

Dishonesty will always come back to hurt you eventually. Make sure that you are up front during interviews with perspective employees about things like pay, student behavior, coaching requirements, and so forth. You can try to trick someone into working for you if you want to, but is the resulting hate and bad will that you will bring on yourself really worth it?

Story Time: I once did a phone interview for a teaching position in another state. It was a conference call setup, with multiple people asking me questions. During the interview, I asked them how the student behavior was at their school. One of the interviewers quickly said, "I am not sure how to answer that." Then another one quickly jumped in with, "We have no behavior problems." (I think it was the principal.) I should have been immediately suspicious, but I decided to accept the position and drove seven hours to move in and get started.

When I got to the school, I asked some of the teachers the same question about student behavior. More than one of them told me that violence regularly occurred at the school. One told me that there were often fights and that I should be prepared to break one up every day. Whoa. Needless to say, I did not stay. So, if you are involved in interviewing potential teachers, be sure that you are always truthful. If your school has less than favorable aspects, own them and admit them. Lying about your school's issues just to fill a position could come back to bite you.

Chapter Eleven

Discipline Myths

There are a lot of beliefs out there about discipline and classroom management that simply aren't true. Who knows how they got started. It is likely that they are either outdated or they come from people who haven't been in a classroom in years, if ever. Don't worry, I am going to set the record straight about these untruths that have been holding back teachers for years.

328. MYTH—Great relationships with students are all the discipline you need.

This myth seems to be gaining steam in recent years, especially among administrators. It goes something along the lines of, "If you just focus on having great relationships with students, then discipline will take care of itself." In a perfect world, maybe this could be true. But you are dealing with kids here, don't forget. Kids are known to misbehave on occasion. Having great relationships with students will sure help, but a wise teacher will still be prepared for those times when everything won't be so lovey-dovey. After all, even the best parents in the world with the best relationships with their children have to discipline every now and then. The same thing is true for teachers.

329. MYTH—Never have more than ten rules.

Rules are a part of life. There are hundreds if not thousands of rules that we encounter in our daily lives: rules for behavior, rules for being socially acceptable, rules for sports, rules that are actual laws. And on and on. They may not all have serious consequences attached to them, but rules are a part of any civilized society. And there are lots of them.

Traditional thinking has often been that having too many rules will just stress out students. This couldn't be further from the truth. As long as the rules and consequences are reasonable and the teacher can explain why they are in place, students will be just fine. Ron Clark, in his book *The Essential 55*, describes his classroom rules covering everything from classroom routines and manners to behavior, and he is one of the best there is at forming great relationships with students. If he can have a lot of rules, so can you. So have as few or as many rules as you want. Just make sure you don't make more than you can keep up with.

330. MYTH—Calling parents will solve your discipline problems.

Teachers have been told forever that a parent phone call should be included as a consequence on any good discipline plan. This is not to say that a call home is an entirely ineffective consequence, but it doesn't pack the same punch that it used to. Maybe it is because kids don't respect their parents like they used to, or maybe parents don't respect teachers like they used to. Who knows. What does seem to be clear is that the threat of a call home will not have much effect on many students these days.

A call home should be used as an informal consequence that you may go to in an effort to get the parents to help. You probably shouldn't count on it having a great impact, though. Sometimes it might work, but it is certainly no guarantee. Consider a successful parent phone call a bonus if it does work. Counting on it as an effective consequence or having it as part of an official discipline plan is probably not a good idea, though.

331. MYTH—You shouldn't smile before Christmas.

This may be the most classic advice in existence that is given to teachers. Believe it or not, this advice is still being given in some college education classes for future teachers. Come on! It is time to move on from this one. Coming in cranky and serious may intimidate your students into behaving well, but there are other ways to go achieve that goal that aren't quite so ugly. Have an organized discipline plan, think of your students like family, and form great relationships and you can smile all you want.

332. MYTH—Veteran teachers are automatically better than young ones.

This is probably not sharing any great revelation to say that this one is not always true. Logic might tell you that the more experience teachers have, the better they will be, but it is easy to see that some veteran teachers are burned out, unmotivated, or just hanging on until retirement. And, of course, there are some really great young teachers out there as well. Experience isn't always everything. Sometimes talent is just talent, no matter the age.

333. MYTH—Teachers should be automatically good at discipline.

Why is it that so many administrators seem to think that as soon as you get your teaching degree, you should instantly be great at classroom management? This just blows my mind. Just because you can teach or got your certification in college doesn't automatically mean you also know how to handle student misbehavior. Come on, people. There are many, many teachers who are great at teaching content but not so great at discipline. If that is you, don't feel bad. This tip is not included to pick on you. Don't be tempted to leave the profession because of it. Just sharpen up those classroom management skills and know that you are not alone.

334. MYTH—There is only one way to have effective discipline in the classroom.

This is definitely a myth. Are there fundamental truths that are required to have great discipline? Sure. But there are many different ways to go about it. Maybe you like to have a lot of official rules and consequences. Maybe you just like to have three general rules about respect, being nice, and so on. The trick is to find what works for you and your personality. Some teachers are just naturals with classroom management and couldn't even really tell you why they are. So explore some of the ideas out there about it and find the best fit for you.

335. MYTH—Good teachers don't sleep much.

Wrong. Get this one out of your head right now. Good teachers take care of their health so they can be at their best. Yes, there occasionally may be times you have to stay up late and work on something. Making a habit of doing this, though, is a fast track to burnout.

336. MYTH—Good teachers *need* coffee.

There are more ways to get energy and focus than just taking a stimulant to get the job done. Ouch. There may be some hurt feelings with this one. Don't talk yourself into believing that you are dependent on the coffee drug to be able to function. This is just not true. You would be surprised how much energy you can get from healthy living. And maybe if you were getting enough sleep, you wouldn't need to take something to get you to wake up.

337. MYTH—Teachers *must* be serious all the time to have effective discipline in the classroom.

This kind of thinking is a good way to burn yourself out. It is no fun to have to force yourself to be serious all day, every day. There are tremendously effective teachers who are serious, mean (gasp!), friendly, silly, cool, nerdy, and on and on. There is no one right way that works for everyone. The secret is to find what fits your personality and make it work. If serious is your thing, go for it. Whatever you do, though, don't drastically change your personality just because you think it will bring results.

338. MYTH—The best way to discipline is to be mean at first and then lighten up.

Hey, why don't you start out a tyrant and then slowly turn up the dial on the niceness meter? Please. There is no need for that kind of manipulation. Be yourself from the beginning. Can you relax a little more once you get a feel for you students and get to know them a little better? Sure. But don't think there is some perfect spectrum of meanness and kindness that has to be carefully followed to be successful.

339. MYTH—Teachers should not talk discipline on the first day of class because it will seem negative.

This one is on my personal hate list but definitely widespread. Why do so many people consider discipline to be a bad word, not to be discussed early on for fear of stressing out the children? Come on. They can handle it. You are better off getting your procedures established before you jump right into content. It doesn't matter how good your lessons are if you don't have order and boundaries established. That is, unless you are one of the about 0.1 percent of teachers who can do whatever they want and still have great classroom management regardless. If that is you, congratulations. You can probably skip this section. And probably write your own book. For the rest of you, feel free to talk a little rules, consequences, and procedures early on, and don't worry about damaging the students' psyches.

340. MYTH—It is impossible to recover from discipline mistakes.

Teachers by nature seem to be a very anxious and fearful group. This may be surprising considering the way many of them act like they are indestructible superheroes in class. A fear that often occurs is that you better be perfect with your classroom management or you will never be able to recover. Talk about placing unnecessary stress on yourself. Are you better off having everything polished and worked out from day one? Sure. But it is not the end of the world if you have to make an adjustment or two along the way. It is not even a total disaster to have to completely redo your discipline plan at some point. While it may not be ideal, you still can make changes to your discipline plan at any time if needed.

341. MYTH—Your student-teaching experience will tell you if a career in teaching is right for you.

Some teachers put the entire weight of their career decision in education on their student-teaching experience. They either left the profession or stayed based on how it went. Yikes. There are too many parts of student teaching that may not carry over to a normal teaching situation. During your time student teaching, for instance, you are completely at the mercy of your host teacher. If that teacher already has established great discipline, you probably won't have much trouble with student misbehavior. The reverse is also true. Yes, student teaching can give you a clue about how well suited you are for teaching. If you hate every minute of it, then you may want to consider doing something else. Just realize that things may be way different once you get out on your own.

342. MYTH—The same rules apply for teachers and students.

You may have heard comments before like "students can't drink soda in class, so the teacher shouldn't be able to drink soda either." "Students can't use their phones in class, so the teacher shouldn't be able to either." This kind of thinking is a breakdown of the idea that the teacher is in charge. When this concept disappears, it is going to be very difficult on teachers to establish the best learning environment possible. There must be a clear understanding that the teacher is the authority and in charge. On a side note, even with this being the case, it is still not wise for teachers to flaunt their authority. Don't rub it in. But let's not make the case that everything should be the same for students and teachers. That is just not realistic.

343. MYTH—Cranky, scary, mean teachers are automatically bad teachers.

As uncomfortable as this may be for some of us to admit, you do not necessarily have to have a Mary Poppins attitude to be a great teacher. Some of my best teachers were cranky (to put it nicely). They were no-nonsense, strict, and very serious. This kind of teacher seems to be a dying breed, but they are the kind who toughen you up. Everyone isn't always going to act like your mother in life. It's best to get used to it early on. If you do aspire to be the cranky-type teacher, just be careful. There is a very fine line between strictness and toughness and just bullying.

Story Time: One of the popular buzzwords in the education world today is "relationship." "Having great relationships with students is the best way to avoid student misbehavior," some say. While it is true that the lovable teacher can be successful, I am not sure that this approach is essential to teaching success. Many of us can remember a teacher or two in our past who was strict and serious, but also great. I know that one of the best teachers I ever had was a middle school math teacher who was humorless, serious, and no-nonsense 100 percent of the time. I had similar teachers in high school who were also great. We all love the fun-loving type teacher, but sometimes the strict ones can be just as impactful.

344. MYTH—It is okay for teachers to break school rules they don't like.

Teachers often love to be in charge. Some may even be accused of being control freaks. They are used to being able to do whatever they want (within reason) and having a lot of power. This isn't always a bad thing if they know where to draw the line. But just deciding not to follow an established school rule because you don't like it is going too far. Yes, teachers, you do have a lot of power. Just remember that it is not unlimited.

345. MYTH—*Discipline* is a bad word.

Sometimes the word gets a bad rap, as if any form of it is bad for kids. Let's not even use the word *discipline* or phrases like "classroom management," some might say. Ugh. Let's stop trying to spoil our kids completely rotten, shall we. Good parents and teachers discipline kids because they love them. It may not always be pleasant, but sometimes a disciplinary action is what is best for a child. Just be sure that you aren't using discipline as a weapon out of frustration or anger. Discipline with the purpose of helping a child is legitimate. Doing it for any other reason is not.

346. MYTH—Failing students are the fault of the teacher.

The process of learning is a group effort. It takes the student, the teacher, and sometimes even parents and peers for learning to take place at the highest level. A failing grade should never be automatically blamed on teachers. Sometimes it may be their fault. Other times it may be entirely the fault of the student. Sometimes it may be a combination of both. But let's not go putting all of the responsibility on the teacher just to have some kind of easy measurement system. This is lazy thinking by administrators, and it just isn't an accurate representation of reality.

347. MYTH—Big, tall, strong men are better at discipline than women.

Wrong. There have been big, burly football-playing types who were run over by their students. There have also been little old ladies under five feet tall who were the best disciplinarians you have ever seen. It's all about the attitude and the methods used. Don't worry about your supposed limitations based on how you look. You can be good at discipline if you want to be.

348. MYTH—Nice teachers will get run over by students.

Niceness or meanness has very little to do with effective discipline. You can be very kind and still be strict and effective with classroom management. Conversely, you can be mean and be terrible at classroom management. Contrary to popular belief, there is no need to bully students into good behavior. There are better ways to do it.

349. MYTH—A great lesson is all the discipline you need.

This is another favorite of administrators, and another one on my hate list. It is yet one more example of taking the easy way out and making things more simplistic than they actually are. Someone may say, "If your lesson was better, the students would behave better!" Ugh. That may be technically true, but teachers shouldn't *always* be expected to have riveting and entertaining lessons. Sometimes students will be required to do things that they just won't like. The answer is not always to improve the lesson. So let's try to get rid of this idea that teachers should just entertain their students into behaving well. Yuck!

350. MYTH—I am good at discipline when I coach, so I will be automatically good at it in the classroom.

If you are a coach, this can be an easy mistake to make. You may be great at discipline when you coach, so you don't think you have to worry about it at all in the classroom. Wrong. There are major differences in the way you handle discipline when coaching versus teaching. When you are coaching, for instance, the kids want to be there. They are much more likely to listen to what you have to say as a result. You also have something they want—playing time. This is a far different situation than having a grade or learning to motivate students.

Not to mention that when you are coaching, you can always use the old go-to discipline strategy of making them run.

Story Time: I coached basketball for most of my teaching career, and I always had confidence in my ability to establish discipline in this setting. I felt like it was one of my biggest strengths as a coach. The classroom, however, was a different story. For some reason, I was only average at best with discipline there. This rang true for me one year when I had a player in class the year after I had coached him. In the basketball setting, he was respectful, well mannered, and a model of good behavior. In the classroom, however, he was a terror. He was one of the worst behaved students I ever had. How could this be? I realized that coaching and teaching situations are very different. So be careful not to assume that your discipline strategies in one area will work the same way in the other.

Chapter Twelve

Coaching

Coaches are teachers too. While their situation and pressures may be different from the classroom teacher, there are still a lot of similarities in what works and doesn't work. Here are a few of my thoughts after spending over a decade in high school coaching.

351. Don't coach anything you never played.

This is not meant to be a hard-and-fast rule, but you may want to think twice before you consider coaching anything that you never played in an organized way. There is something about being able to relate to your players after having been in the same situations that they will be facing that is important.

352. Don't kiss up to your star players.

Different players have different roles on your team. Some play every minute of every game and score a lot of points, and some barely play at all. The best coaches value every player for what he or she contributes, regardless of what that role may be. Be very careful about giving special treatment to your star players or letting them get away with things that you wouldn't let other players do. That is a good way to lose your team.

353. Plan your practices to the minute.

You only get so much time to practice, so value every minute like it is precious and plan your practices accordingly. Running your practices by winging it will not only waste time but can also keep you from covering everything that needs attention.

354. Be on time.

Players appreciate a coach who respects their time. Make it a goal to start every practice when you say you will, and don't keep your players waiting. Whether it is true or not, starting your practices late sends the message that you don't really take what you are doing seriously.

355. End your practices when you say you will.

Practices can be tough, especially if they are done right. Your players will resent you if you don't end when you say that you will, though. Not ending on time may also disrespect parents who are expecting to be able to pick up their child at the time you promised. Nothing you do is such an emergency that it can't wait a day. If it is that important, maybe you should be planning your practices more efficiently (see tip #353).

356. Have a very organized discipline plan.

There are just about as many discipline styles as there are coaches. Some are strict disciplinarians, some are loose and casual. And others are everything in between. Many dramatically different styles have been effective. How you run your discipline for your team is important, but equally important is knowing exactly how you want to go about it.

357. Be friendly with other coaches.

Coaching is like a brotherhood (or sisterhood). Don't be the coach who is too good to be friendly with other coaches because of some weird competitive or paranoid issue.

358. Respect the referees.

There is no excuse for being hateful to referees. First of all, refereeing is extremely difficult. They make mistakes just like anyone else does. If you aren't perfect yourself, it might make sense to be a little more forgiving. And second, do you really think that bullying referees helps you get future calls? Even if it did, do you really want to have to rely on being a bully to get results?

359. Work for free if you have to.

How badly do you want to be a successful coach? If you really want to make it big in coaching, you will likely have to make some sacrifices. That might mean working summer camps, taking less than desirable jobs early on to get experience, or even working for free for a little while. If you want to succeed badly enough, you will do whatever it takes.

360. Study innovative plays.

Don't just be satisfied running the plays that you ran during the good old days when you played. There are a lot of great coaches out there who have shared some of their secrets, so why not take advantage of it? I'm not saying that you need a phonebook-sized playbook or that you should be obsessed with finding the holy grail of plays, just keep an eye on things that the most successful coaches are doing.

361. Don't worry about fancy drills.

Coaches love drills. Some drills are definitely better than others. While you may want to keep an eye on learning some new methods, it is probably more important to try to perfect the ones you have. If you aren't happy with the drills you use, by all means make some changes. Just don't go on a journey for the perfect drills that will win you a championship. They do not exist.

362. Plan team-bonding activities.

Go out to eat. See if you can have a parent cook a meal for the team. Go to church or the movies. Teams who connect off the field or court often play better together.

363. Don't let parents come to practices.

Sometimes there are things that coaches and players do that should be kept between them. Keep the parents out of practices unless you want to open up the door to meddling and distractions.

364. Don't let your players talk to or listen to people in the stands (including parents).

As the saying goes, if you listen to people in the stands, you will soon join them. Insist that your players keep their focus on what they are doing. This is good advice for yourself too.

365. Support the other sports teams at your school.

Be a team player. Don't think you or your sport is better than others at your school. Support the other sports and they will probably support you. Coaching life is much more pleasant when coaches at a school are working together instead of against each other.

Conclusion

So there you have it—all the tips you need to become a better educator. Like I said in the preface, I know how hard teaching can be. It can make you crazy at times, but it is a noble profession. I will always be a friend to those who sacrifice and dedicate themselves to the cause of helping young people make a better life for themselves.

Happy teaching,
Doug

About the Author

Doug Campbell grew up in Germany, Florida, California, and Belgium as part of a military family. He graduated from Furman University in Greenville, South Carolina, with a BA and a master's in education, and he still lives in South Carolina. He has over twenty years of high school teaching experience in South Carolina and North Carolina, teaching everything from US history and economics to AP calculus and other math classes at the high school level. During the past five years, he has been devoted to helping teaching excel, survive, and overcome the variety of challenges that often come with a career in education. He created WithoutAnger.com (now EducatorTips.com) to help teachers improve their skills in discipline, classroom management, success, and general survival in the education profession.

www.ingramcontent.com/pod-product-compliance
Lightning Source LLC
Chambersburg PA
CBHW021759230426
43669CB00006B/129